MIDDLE SCHOOL

PARENTS' COOPERATIVE

SCHOOL

ROOM 11

MRS. SWIST

Experiencing art in the elementary school

Experiencing art in the elementary school

George F. Horn
*Supervisor of Art
Baltimore City Public
Schools, Maryland*

and

Grace Sands Smith
*Formerly, Director, Art Education
Houston Public Schools, Texas*

Co-published in Texas by
Hendrick-Long Publishing Company, Dallas, Texas
and Davis Publications, Inc., Worcester, Massachusetts

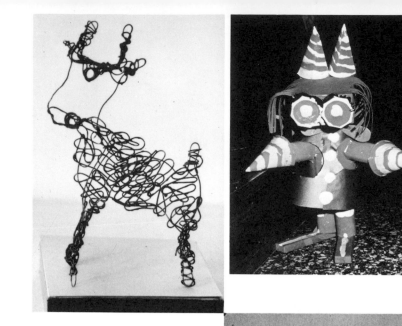

Copyright 1971

Davis Publications, Inc.
Worcester, Massachusetts, U.S.A.
Library of Congress Catalog Card Number: 70-135743
ISBN 0-87192-036-0
Second Printing 1972

Printing: Davis Press, Inc.
Type: Univers Medium
Graphic Design: George F. Horn

Contents

Cover: *Mural, colored tissue and felt markers. A group project by seven-year-old children, Houston Independent School District, Texas. Virginia Rayburn, teacher.*

Tempera painting, kindergarten, age 5.

To the teacher

In today's world of science and technology, often characterized by an emphasis on conformity and material well-being, the art experience provides a much-needed humanizing balance in the life of the child. It is through the arts that it is possible for the inner spirit — the unique voice of the child — to seek and to find the satisfaction and enjoyment that accompanies the urgent quest for self-expression.

Experiencing art in the elementary school should be an adventure — an opening of doors that will broaden the boundaries of the child's world and nurture his creative and imaginative capabilities. It should accommodate the child's natural capacity for delight and wonder and his joy of personal accomplishment as he reflects upon his own world, searches for new meanings with materials and discovers self.

This book presents a continuous, sequential program of art, beginning with the simpler skills and understandings and progressing to the more complex. It encourages a qualitative rather than a quantitative encounter with art and challenges the child to a higher level of esthetic sensitivity. At each grade level, appropriate emphasis is placed upon THE WORLD OF THE ARTIST, OUR ENVIRONMENT and CREATIVE ART ACTIVITIES.

The ultimate success of the art experience for the elementary school child rests upon you, for you have the distinct role of leading, inspiring and encouraging the child toward high achievement. The enthusiasm that you project, your concern for the child, your search for new ideas, your dedication to the task of teaching and your own active pursuit of excellence will assure a satisfying and worthwhile experience in the visual arts for the child.

G.F.H. and G.S.S.

"How I felt on Christmas", tempera painting, age 6.

EXPERIENCING ART IN THE ELEMENTARY SCHOOL

Painting, age 10.

Self-expression, discovery, fulfillment

"My picture is about a brown and white spotted cow I saw while taking a trip. I have always thought how much fun it would be to milk a cow. Since I couldn't milk one in real life, I enjoyed painting a make-believe picture in my art class."

The most enjoyable and meaningful time in the young child's life can be his early experiences with various plastic materials that allow him to express his ideas in a spontaneous, visual way — paints and crayons, brilliant colors; ink and a discarded spool;

yarn and burlap; a ball of clay that can be rolled, smashed, cut, joined, shaped and reshaped; boxes of all sizes that can be modified, painted, and combined to represent a sparkling new city or an unusual animal. Completely involved and characteristically unrepressed, the child achieves an enormous sense of satisfaction as he uses various art materials to give visual dimension to his thoughts, ideas, and imagination. He thrills to the excitement of discovery as he brings a large paint-laden brush into contact with a blank piece of paper and makes his very own mark. He proudly surveys the lump of clay that he has transformed into a symbol of his pet dog — or of the massive rhinoceros that he saw on his recent visit to the zoo. And the mosaic mural that is now permanently installed on the corridor wall, right outside of the principal's office, adds to his feeling of accomplishment. He didn't create the entire mosaic but he did apply many of the small ceramic tiles as he worked with several of his classmates in this group project.

Experiencing art is vital to the child as he becomes more aware of himself and his environment. It opens up new vistas, new doors, new ways for him to say something — something of consequence to him about what he has seen or imagined, or heard, or has done, or would like to do. Art offers the unique opportunity for the child to express his feelings — visually, perceptively, sensitively in a child-like way as he observes, investigates, selects, organizes, appreciates, and discovers new ways to communicate an idea — as he avidly pursues this visual form of creative expression adapting it to his personal interests and needs.

Mask, age 11.

Mosaic, group project, ages 9-11.

Experiencing art is vital to the child.

One Main Place, part of a multi-million dollar urban renewal complex, Dallas, Texas.

Visual awareness, perception, discriminating taste

Equally important to performance activities in the elementary school art program is the conditioning of the child to a critical awareness of his visual environment: the physical components of the world in which he lives and moves — his home, school, church, the shopping center, streets, signs, billboards, buildings, the museum, parks, trees, the farm, animals, rocks; smokestacks, smoke and pollution; demolition and renewal; television. This infinite world of natural and man-made objects is a persistent influence on the child and his growing ability to differentiate beauty from ugliness; good design from that which is inferior. From this environment, where esthetics often appear to be a paradox, the child forms the basis for what he likes, dislikes, selects, rejects — for his own eventual measure of discriminating taste.

The quality of the child's visual and esthetic awareness and of his response to the art experience is directly related to his expanding concept of design. Although the fundamentals of design are not as essential to the child who is in an early stage of visual development, some of the simpler terms or concepts such as color, shape, movement, painting, printmaking, sculpture, should be introduced, discussed, and added to as the child matures. Thus, by the time he reaches the upper level of elementary school, he should have a thorough understanding of basic design concepts and art terminology and how they relate to his environment, to the art of man, and to his personal creative expression.

Free Flow, stainless steel sculpture by Jose de Rivera and located in main lobby of Statler Hilton Hotel, Dallas, Texas.

Appreciation, understanding, enjoyment

Another essential facet of the art program in the elementary schools is bringing the child into a meaningful understanding of the art of man, both past and present — introducing works of art (repro-

ductions, films, filmstrips, the museum) selected on the basis of the child's age level and interest and programmed as a regular part of the art experience. The younger child is delighted by works of art that are colorful, tell a story, or bear some relationship to his own experience. To him, subject matter is important — birds, animals, people, holidays, the circus. But even at this early age level, simple design concepts such as color to create mood, contrasts in sizes of shapes to develop interest, different tempos of movement, and basic ideas (the artist painted those things that interested him and that were familiar to him) should be discussed in relationship to specific art works.

As the child matures the study of works of art should become a more formalized part of the art program with increasing consideration given to:

- art as a product of the society in which it was created. For example, the contrasts between

Man Leaning Against a Wall of Doors, plaster sculpture by George Segal and in collection of Yonkers' Hudson River Museum.
Photo courtesy Geigy Chemical Corporation.

Primitive art, Greek art, and Op and Pop of the 1960s; Egyptian Pyramid, Gothic Cathedral, and today's glass and steel skyscrapers.

- the influence on the artist of religion, politics, and the specific civilization.

- the influence of the artist at different times in history; i.e. the impact on society today of the industrial designer, stylist, fashion artists, TV advertising artist.

- subject matter in art.

- style or mode of interpretation utilized by the artist (Realism in contrast to Impressionism, Cubism, Expressionism, Surrealism, Abstract Expressionism).

- the visual elements (line, shape, mass, space, color, value, texture) and how the artist, architect, designer, craftsman used or uses these elements to give shape to his ideas — to produce the qualities of unity, balance, movement, simplicity and harmony in his art work.

- tools, materials, techniques, and processes of the artist — the influence of science and technology.

In today's world the child is continually surrounded by thousands of images — television, films, books, magazines, advertisements, displays, the total environment. Some of these images are good; many are bad. Bringing the child into contact with art and design that touches on every aspect of man's life will help him to acquire a broader and deeper understanding of the visual arts, will enable him to speak the language of art, and will assist him toward becoming more selective and discriminating in his own taste. This expanding program of art appreciation, based on the interests and levels of understanding of the maturing child, can also be a tremendous source of pleasure and joy for the child, the teacher and parents.

All That is Beautiful, serigraph by Ben Shahn, 20th Century American. Photo courtesy Baltimore Museum of Art.

Brush and paint, age 5.

Stitchery and appliqué wall hanging, age 10.

Visual, esthetic, and creative maturity

Experiencing art in the elementary schools assures that the child is growing visually and becoming more perceptive; that he is developing the ability to think critically; that he is acquiring a meaningful understanding of fundamental design concepts and qualities; that he is relating these design concepts to his personal visual response through creative problem-solving; that he is becoming more proficient in his use of art tools and materials; that he is becoming aware of and conversant about his cultural heritage; that he is growing more sensitive to his environment (natural and man-made) and developing his thinking about ways to improve the esthetic quality of his surroundings.

To be effective the elementary school art program must be organized around the needs, interests and capabilities of the child at different age levels and in relation to his stage of creative growth and development. Variations in the type of graphic expression (scribbling, symbolism, concern for detail, realism) that can be expected at different age and grade levels — even within a single age level — result from varying rates of physical, perceptual, and mental growth; varying social and economic backgrounds; attitudes of adults; traditions, values; and earlier opportunities for creative expression that the child may have had.

The elementary school art program that will ultimately produce visual, esthetic, and creative maturity in the child should:

1. Consist of continuous learning experiences that include two- and three-dimensional art activities, progressing from the simpler, direct use of materials for the young child to the more complex involvement of the older child.

2. Provide frequent and regular opportunity for the child to experiment with materials, explore ideas, and discover new techniques and processes that may be utilized in his personal visual expression.

3. Assure a broadening relationship of the child to art content and understandings that will enable him to use correct art terminology that he may speak effectively and knowingly about his art and the art of others; to know what art is, what it means to him; to describe, analyze, criticize; to perceive and relate his observations with an appropriate response.

4. Provide time for the child to observe and become

familiar with art works of today as well as of other civilizations.

5. Allow time for the child just to look and SEE things around him, natural and man-made : a tree, a leaf, branches, twigs, the trunk, bark. What is a tree in the summer? How does its appearance change in the winter? Or does it?

Repeat print, age 10.

Chalk drawing, age 9.

6. Develop the child's skills in handling tools, in selecting materials for specific purposes, and in utilizing techniques and art processes that are appropriate for his creative response to a particular art problem.

7. Encourage the child toward a realization of his potential for self-expression and the joy and satisfaction that results.

8. Expand the child's emerging self-identification with his artistic product and enrich the total learning process.

Silk screen print, age 10.

The child and his visual response

Art — process and product

Experiencing art means something different to each child and his graphic efforts reflect quite candidly his stage of personal visual development. For whatever his visual configuration may be it is the sum of his capability to perceive and to conceptualize through art materials available to him at any given moment in the process of his growing physically, mentally, intellectually, socially, and perceptually. Thus the child sees, thinks, imagines, recalls, searches as he formulates concepts on which his visual response is based.

Scribbles and symbols of the very young child, often incomprehensible — even discounted by adults — are significant manifestations that mark the child's earliest efforts to visualize an idea. In this sense, the art process is a major educational contributor to the child's growth and development; to his ultimate personality and sense of security; and to his forming of vital motor skills. Even more important to the young child, the scribbles and symbols are his — and stand as dynamic and direct statements of his own small world. As the child grows perceptually and becomes more sophisticated in his conceptualizing, he achieves a capability for greater complexity in his creative expression — in his response to the art experience. At all age levels and in all stages of the child's visual development, an essential motivating force is the encouragement given to the child by teachers, parents, and other adults. Positive reinforcement founded on that which may be expected at various age levels (not on adult standards of evaluation) will assist the child in his transformation from utilizing art as a purely communicative experience to finding in art a natural and appropriate (for him) form of graphic expression.

Painting, age 6.

Crayon drawing, age 6.

Papier-mâché animals, age 8.

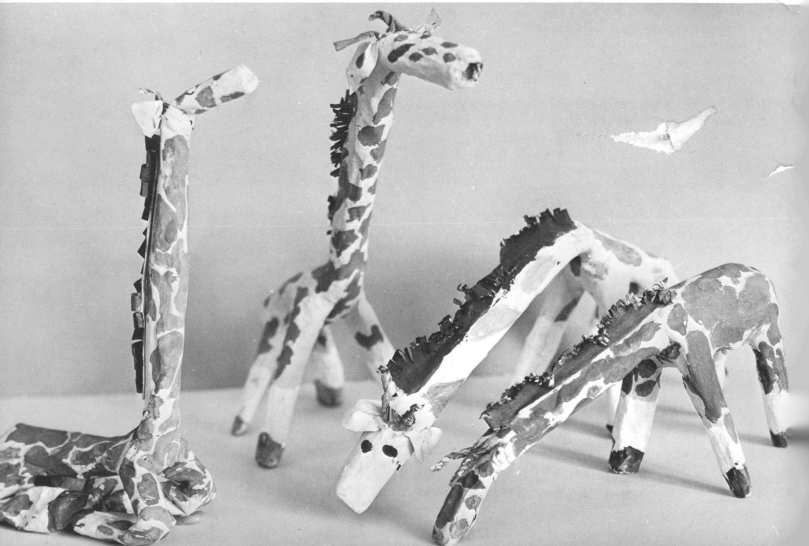

Motivation, inspiration, stimulation

The young child is a vital, lively, active, imaginative, puzzling, impulsive, growing being. He has a natural capacity for producing personal visual imagery; for becoming critical, perceptive, analytical, aware; for developing the ability to differentiate between order and disorder, good design and bad design; for appreciating and enjoying. He is innately curious and directs much of his attention toward inquiring, collecting, examining, searching, discovering.

Encouragement, guidance, and acceptance by the teacher and other adults, particularly parents, is essential. The child's continuing interest in art experiences is nurtured by a sincere understanding on the part of adults; by listening intently as he talks about himself, his friends (pets and animals included), his ideas, his dreams, his discoveries — his birthday party, the boy next door, George the cat; the odd-shaped, rough-textured, flat pebble that he found on the way to school. The child's level of enthusiasm is furthered by having interesting and varied art materials readily available to him; by opening new and wondrous doors that lead to fresh and exhilarating experiences; by surrounding him with an environment of excitement — color, things, prints, illustrations, sounds, textured items that elicit touch and handling.

The child shapes his art work by what he knows, by his imagination and his world of fantasy, and by his spirited child-like perceptiveness.

1. THE CHILD AND HIS PERSONAL EXPERIENCES

His home — the front door, backyard, his room, the kitchen. The community in which he lives — the school, his church, streets. What is seen on the street — sidewalks, curbs, broken curbs, telephone poles, lights, TV antennas on rooftops, the traffic signal, buildings being demolished, new buildings, stores, stores at Christmas time. Carnivals, fairs, circuses. Winter, spring, summer, and fall in town. On the farm — a tractor, animals. A ranch — cowboys, corrals, the feed lot. Windmills, rice mills, oil derricks. A freight train. Rainy days, dry days, hot days. The zoo — lions, tigers, a porcupine. Trees, plants, flowers of all colors, weeds, rocks, streams, the creek, the sky, the wind blowing hard. People — policemen, firemen, the Good Humor man, old folks, not-so-old folks, family, friends, playmates. Games, sports, jumping, leaping, hopping, skipping, running.

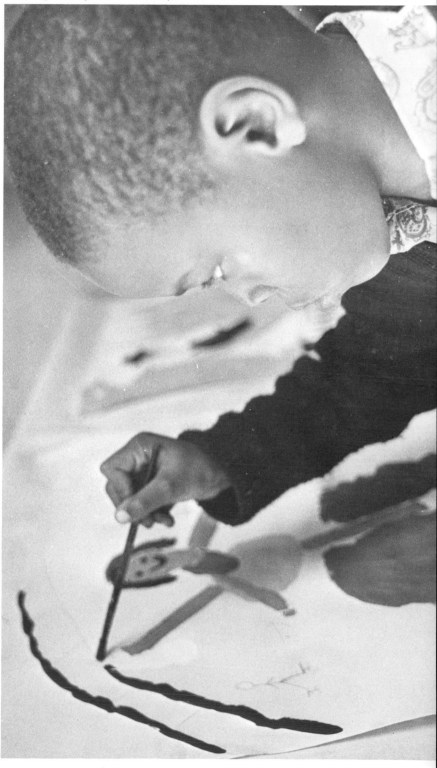

Encouragement, guidance and acceptance are essential.

Many more items could be added to this list of experiences in the child's life. He may bring a very precious (to him) toy animal to school to show to his classmates. This could become the basis for an exciting lesson on making toy animals from boxes of various sizes and shapes, paint, paper, yarn, spools, buttons; or simple but imaginative cloth puppets that would befriend the toy animal and converse with it; or perhaps the toy animal would agree to model so that the children could paint its portrait.

Art activities based on the child's experiences and from the viewpoint of the child can be of tremendous interest to him. Use these experiences as bases for visual expression. Have the child talk about his world: ask leading questions; show enthusiasm; broaden the discussion by displaying illustrations or a reproduction of a familiar painting that relates. Be sure to have the necessary art materials ready and allow sufficient time for their use.

Tempera painting, age 11.

2. THE CHILD AND HIS IMAGINATION

The child is an imaginative creature and characteristically inclined to the world of fantasy, the unknown, and the unreal. This source of motivation for his graphic expression may be encouraged through poems, stories, story-telling, music. Unusual topics that stretch the imagination often result in fanciful and capricious but delightfully fresh responses. For example, *a trip to outer space or to the moon;* what kind of creature could be lurking behind the rim of a crater? Or, *a ball that bounces high over the rooftops and goes on a journey;* what does it see?

Accessibility of unusual materials stimulates the fanciful in the mind's eye of the child: scrap materials, found objects, odd-shape pieces of wood, a wide assortment of discarded boxes. Materials such as these challenge the child as he seeks ways to organize them to give visual shape to a whimsical idea.

Puppets, age 8.

Tempera painting, age 7.

Diorama, age 9.

3. THE CHILD AND CREATING FROM DIRECT OBSERVATION

Help the child to SEE: himself, his friends, the physical environment around him; the shape and structure of things, colors, textures, action, movement; to become perceptive and to grow in awareness. This is stimulating to the child as he experiences art. As his vision and sensitivity to life expand, he has more to enthuse about — a broader and more varied source of personal ideas for painting, sculpture, printmaking, and other art activities. Bringing the child into a more extensive, perceptive, and knowledgeable relationship with his world is in itself a motivating factor as he responds graphically to the art program. Providing him with more confidence as he selects and manipulates materials to give form to ideas. For older children in particular, sketching trips in the vicinity of the school, to a farm or zoo, to the shopping center or a weather-beaten old building, can be exciting and contribute to the art learning experience. Then too, drawing each other and drawing interesting objects in the classroom can be equally useful and appealing to the child.

Art experiences based on direct observation develop visual keenness — encourage the child to SEE. As the child grows, his searching mind tells him that there is something he must know about the structure of things in order for him to be "right" in his visual statement. He studies his own art work with a critical eye and raises questions. "What is wrong with the figure? The arms appear too short and they don't seem to bend right. Why doesn't the figure look like it is running? The roof and the windows in the house don't go together! What can I do about it?" Vague answers to these incisive questions will not suffice.

Discuss proportions of the figure. Have a child pose — standing, walking, bending, jumping — while others sketch. Take the children outside to SEE a house. Discuss the shape, size, and space relationships of the component parts of the house — windows, doors, porch, steps, roof. Provide time for the children to sketch on the scene. Talk about structure, form, proportion, color, texture, movement, action as they relate.

Have the children bring natural and man-made objects (bark, twigs, shells, dried weeds, rocks, found objects, a toy, a discarded kitchen utensil) into the classroom for further observation, study, and to be used possibly as subject matter in drawing and painting.

Prepare a special place in the room for a continuous
display of objects that may be touched, handled —
objects that arouse curiosity and add to the child's
growing concepts of color, texture, form, design.
Reproductions of paintings or sculpture that relate to
the objects may be displayed to give greater educational and visual impact.

Trip to the zoo for motivation.

Figure composition from student models.

Figure drawing composition based on student models.

4. THE CHILD AND THE MEDIUM FOR VISUAL EXPRESSION

A tremendous source of inspiration for the child in his visual expression is found in the medium or the materials associated with his art experience. Although a limited understanding (direct use) of certain art materials such as paints, crayons, and clay will be satisfying to the very young child, repetition in the way materials are used can become a boring chore in itself. Opportunities should be provided for experimentation that will assist the child toward discovering new and unusual qualities in art materials and how these discoveries may be applied to his own creative expression.

The art program at all age levels involves the child in problem-solving, design decisions, selection and use of materials (two- and three-dimensional), tools, processes, techniques. A fundamental difference between age levels is the degree to which the child is involved and the relative complexity of art problems and materials. The developmental level of the child (his interests and previous art experiences) are factors upon which selection of art content and materials are based.

The child's experience in art expression can be enhanced by introducing new ways (to the child) for using the same art materials. Perhaps it is the unpredictable associated with a new technique that helps sustain the enthusiastic and creative spirit of the child. Or, it may be the feeling of adventure as the child discovers the potential and unanticipated result of a new approach to painting or to drawing or building a sculptured form.

Paper sculpture, age 11.

Consider the possibilities with a rather common elementary school art material — the wax crayon. It is quite natural for the very young child to use crayons in a direct manner to make his mark. As he matures, his early excitement and sense of accomplishment can be maintained as he discovers that other unusual and often amusing things happen when he:

- combines crayon with transparent watercolor.
- rubs crayon over the surface of a piece of paper under which textured materials have been placed.
- etches into a paper that has been coated heavily with layers of wax crayons.
- makes a print from a crayon prepared plate.
- melts different colors of crayon in a muffin tin and applies them to paper in liquid form or to cloth to create a batik — a textile design technique developed by Indonesian and Javanese artists. The design is made on the cloth with wax, followed by immersing the cloth in dye. The wax is removed by placing the cloth between layers of paper and pressing with a warm iron. The areas covered by wax reject the dye colors.
- uses solvents such as kerosene with crayon to produce subtle blends in his drawing.

Another example of programming art materials to maintain the interest of the child and to guide him into new levels of visual expression may be illustrated through modeling activities. Earlier experiences may provide the child opportunity to handle, squeeze, pull, cut, push together, and poke clay to find out what it is all about. As he grows and becomes more

Batik design, age 9.

Wood scraps, age 8.

Rubbings and collage, age 10.

skillful, specific techniques such as the pinch pot and coil building method should be introduced. Later, slab construction and various combinations should be added, along with a variety of techniques for surface decoration of clay-built objects.

By programming art materials and art processes — from a relatively simple, limited, direct use for the very young child to a more complex and sophisticated involvement for the older child — art experiences achieve a high degree of stimulation at each level of the child's progress toward maturity.

Cut paper and paste, age 6.

5. THE CHILD AND MOTIVATION THROUGH INSTRUCTIONAL MATERIALS

The child responds to appropriate visual, auditory, kinesthetic, and sensory media. Such instructional and motivational materials assist him in formulating concepts that are related to his graphic expression. Films, filmstrips, slides, tapes, recordings, reproductions, photographs, television, books, periodicals, objets d'art, models should be integrated with performance activities to enrich the child's visual perception, his observation, his conceptualizing, and the heightening of his knowledge of the art process. For the young child, a reproduction of a painting will have appeal not in relation to its historic significance but because of the familiar subject matter, lively colors, or the story it tells him. In a sequential program where the works of the artist, designer, architect, and craftsman of the past and present play an important part, it is possible to build and expand the child's concepts of art and of design. Thus, the more mature child will have the capability for understanding the impact of art on society throughout history; the influence of government, politics, religion, events, and everyday living on the artist; the outstanding eras of civilization that gave birth to various shapes and forms of art. A continuous and expanding association with the many facets of art through such media as suggested here will have major influence on the child's personal and esthetic development and his continuing interest in art as a form of creative expression.

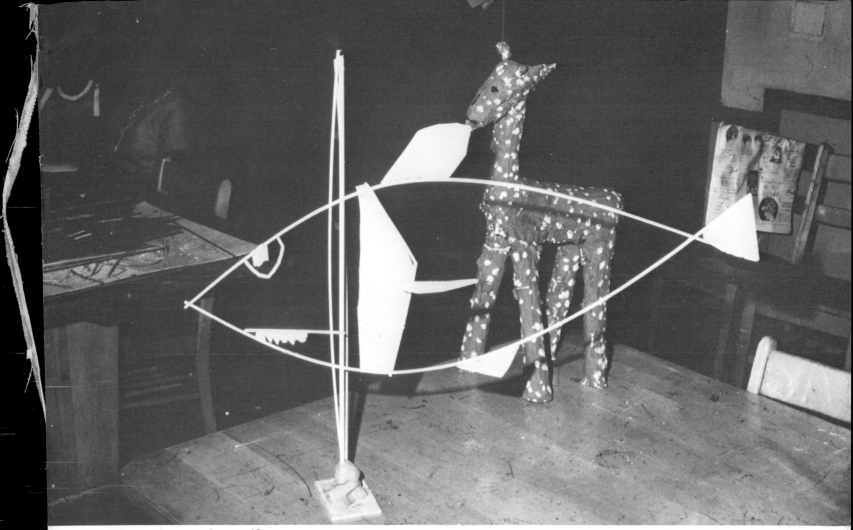

Balsa wood construction, age 10.

Tempera painting, age 11.

31

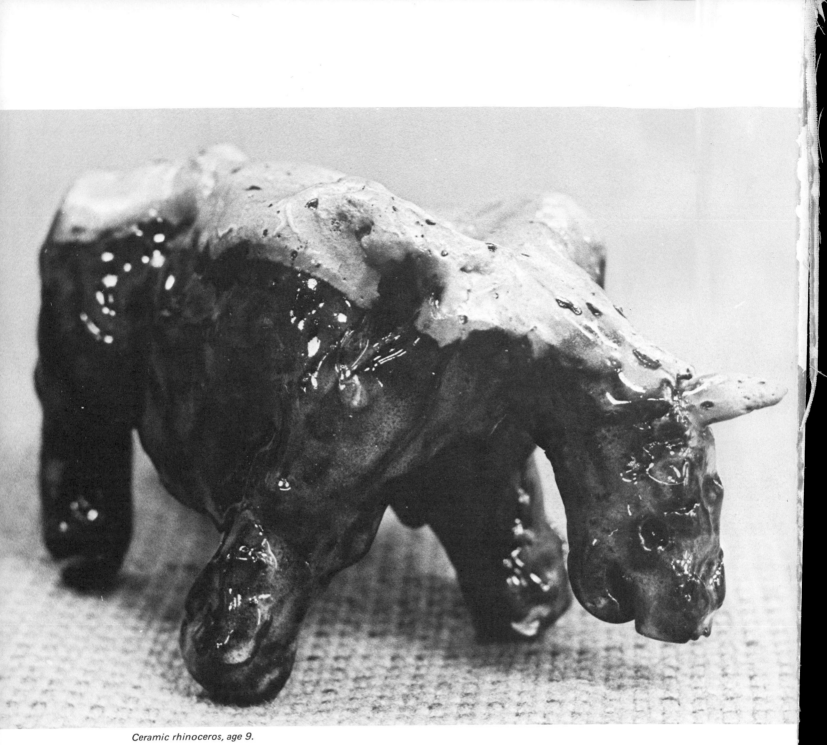

Ceramic rhinoceros, age 9.

Tempera painting, age 6.

Children SEE design in simple, ever-present things that adults seldom notice. They bring to class treasures of curiosity:

- a small green hop toad with bumps on its back.
- prickly cockleburs and multi-colored flowers.
- a flat rock that looks like a pancake.
- a piece of glass that reflects its brilliant hue on a face filled with excitement.

The shape and pattern of clouds.

An insect covered with bright specks of color and displaying two vibrating antennae is fascinating to children. To catch a butterfly is a supreme triumph.

Through these natural discoveries children experience different sensations of color, shape, and texture. The thrill that is generated is a natural motivation for leading them to DISCOVER DESIGN.

Design is not limited to the few things listed here. Design is everywhere — in nature: a stream, a lake, a tree, the sky; and in *man-made objects:* a tall building, a bridge, automobiles, toys and bicycles, a painting and a piece of sculpture. The DISCOVERY of design enhances the joy of LOOKING and of LIVING. The DISCOVERY of design is an unending adventure.

The flow of water over rocks in a stream — and the surrounding textures, patterns and forms.

The massive form of a building. Morris Mechanic Theater, Baltimore, Maryland. M.E. Warren, photographer.

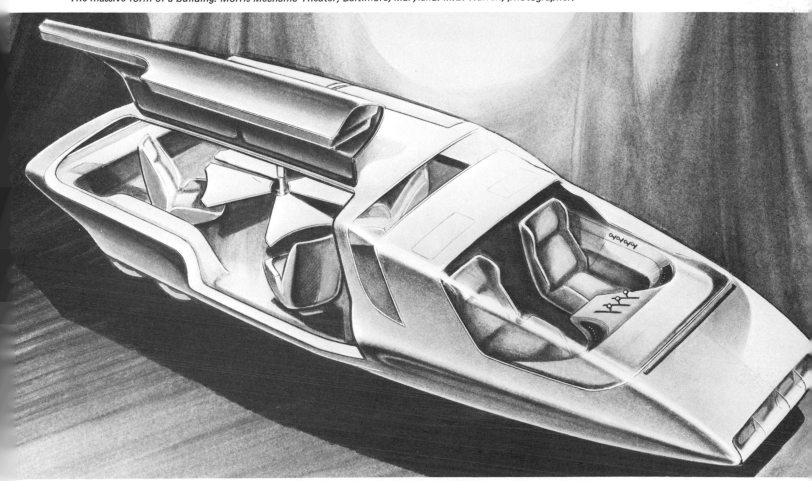

Simplicity of design and streamlined form of a car of the future. Photograph courtesy General Motors Corporation.

Design is organization. It is the specific plan by which something is created or made. Design is the integration of line, color, texture, form, and space that gives visibility and uniqueness to natural or man-made objects. The cocklebur, mentioned earlier, is oval in shape, pale green, and covered with spines that give it a prickly texture. How does this differ from the appearance of a sea shell, the Eiffel Tower, or the painting of a ballet dancer by Degas? Disparate as these examples seem, each represents a special organization and all three contain the same design elements.

The basic tools of the artist, the designer, and the craftsman are the visual elements — *line, form, color, texture, space* — and the ways in which they may be used to produce quality and interest in an art product. An understanding of these design elements and principles is essential to the child's growing awareness and appreciation of art and the environment as well as to his own creative work. However, they should not be taught in a formal, abstract way.

Texture, form and space are dominant in this bronze sculpture, Momento del Volo by Quinto Ghermandi. Southern Methodist University collection.

Through inspiration, challenge, and contact with many good examples of design, natural and man-made, the children should be encouraged to search out and identify visual elements and qualities by looking, touching, smelling, comparing, and experimenting. Children respond eagerly and imaginatively to sensory experiences. A six-year-old stood at the edge of a dazzling bed of hyacinths and exclaimed, "It smells like a purple popsicle".

Design elements and principles interrelate and cannot be isolated and treated without consideration for each other. Line may be an outstanding characteristic of a drawing but shape will also be evident. If crayons are being used, color will be important. However, for the purpose of strengthening child concepts, a special emphasis may be placed upon single visual elements or principles. For example, a discussion of texture along with the opportunity for the children to handle and feel objects of varying textures (paper, wood, bark, fur, cotton, etc.) will assure that the word *texture* will take on concrete meaning for the children. Soon they will be texturing their own work as a result of this meaningful experience.

The following discussion of the visual elements is included specifically for the guidance of the teacher.

Line

There are many kinds of line. A crayon or pen moving across the paper produces a line that may culminate in a scribble. It may define a shape or eventually depict subject matter. Line is also represented by yarn used in stitchery and weaving; by the wire bent to form a piece of sculpture; or it may be incised into a piece of clay as a part of the surface decoration. Many other materials may be used to create linear qualities in a drawing, painting, print, or three-dimensional form.

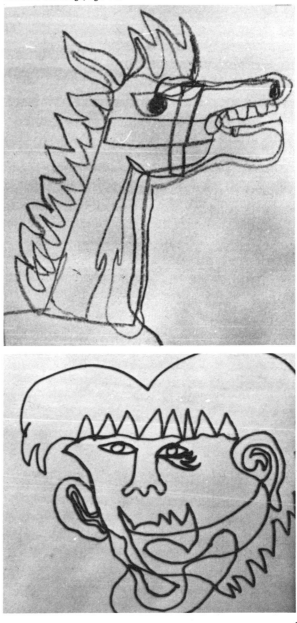

Gesture drawings, age 11.

37

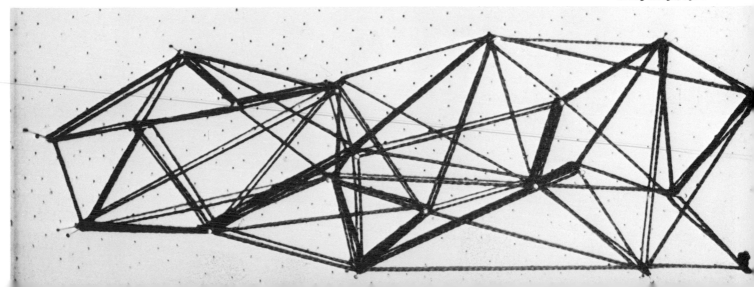

String design, age 9.

Preschool children make scribble drawings of line over line as they enjoy the rhythm of moving their hand and crayon. During kindergarten and the first grade, the line drawings begin to assume symbolic meaning for the child. The same kind of experience occurs when children use their fingers or a stick and draw designs in sand and mud; or chalk on a street or sidewalk.

Line can be thick or thin, precisely drawn, ragged, bold, delicate, timid, light, dark, solid, broken and used to create a variety of moods and effects. Horizontal lines produce a feeling of rest and tranquillity; vertical lines, soaring height and strength; diagonal lines, darting speed, emotion, conflict, excitement. Curved lines are graceful.

The innate qualities of the tools or materials used influence the kind of line that results (pen and ink, brush and paint, crayon, chalk, the edge of a piece of cardboard dipped in paint, a stick and ink, etc.)

The artist uses line to interpret an idea, to create interest, to achieve movement and unity in his work. Looking at a painting, the eyes will involuntarily follow the contour line of shapes or see deep into the picture plane, influenced by the converging lines of a road or a fence or a line of trees. The skillful use of line by the artist transforms the two-dimensional canvas into an illusion of distance and depth.

Assist the children toward a discovery of the many kinds of lines that exist in the local environment — line that may be seen in tree branches, tall bending grass, wires strung atop telephone poles or high-tension electric towers, television antennas, the edges of buildings. Show examples of paintings, prints, sculpture, and architecture in which line is dominant.

Crayon drawing, age 6. Line used to create texture and to define shapes.

Line used to create pattern in this
drawing by Paul Klee, 20th Century Swiss.
Blanche Adler Collection,
Baltimore Museum of Art.

Tempera painting, age 5. Bold use of line
to strengthen figure.

Form (shape, mass, volume)

Everything in nature and in man-made production has a form. Whether the object is a shape on paper which has been made by drawing a line to enclose a shape, or a solid mass of color in a painting, or the three-dimensional volume of a clay sculpture, the identity of each is a specific form.

In the early part of the twentieth century, many promising painters, sculptors, architects, and designers became intent on defining form in new ways. Their exploration led to the development of cubism, abstractionism, futurism, non-objectivism, and many other variants of form-oriented schools of design and painting. They did experimental work in analyzing and converting natural shapes into the geometrical forms they most closely resembled.

The influence of this new definition of form has had a dramatic impact on modern painting, sculpture, architecture, industrial design, furniture and textile design, advertising and poster art; in fact on all aspects of the visual arts.

Children can be guided to be conscious of the shape of things. We have already seen that primary children tend to draw and paint in a partly geometrical way. This is their *natural* way to draw.

Children should not be asked to think about the shapes they are drawing or painting. This tends to confuse them. While working on a picture let them be free to compose it in their own way. However, as they discuss the shape and form of things in the classroom and around the school, their concepts of these visual elements will become clearer. This will be expressed in their paintings at their own speed of comprehension.

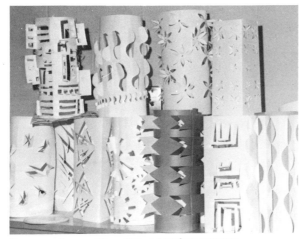

Cut paper forms with sculptured surface patterns.

Harlequin with Accordion by Jacques Lipchitz, 20th Century American sculptor; bronze, height 26''. Courtesy Baltimore Museum of Art.

Sculptured form of a contemporary home perched on top of a lofty mountain; Charles Deaton, architect, Denver, Colorado.

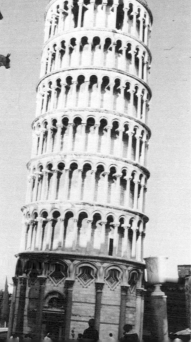

An old familiar form—the Leaning Tower of Pisa.

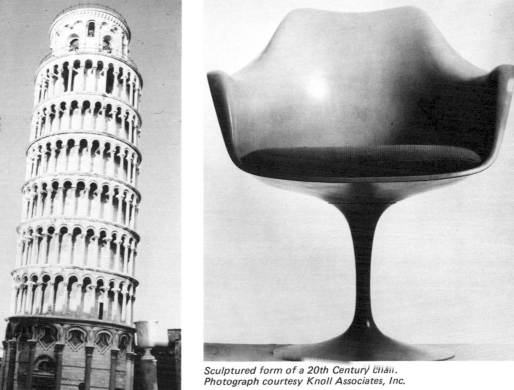

Sculptured form of a 20th Century chair. Photograph courtesy Knoll Associates, Inc.

Child art is characterized by the spontaneous, intuitive use of color.

Color

Color is the element of design that evokes more response than all of the others combined simply because it is color! There are moments for everyone when the magnificence of color is more than they can comprehend. All of the senses are suddenly immersed in breath-taking beauty. The human response to color, in its emotional and psychological aspects, is a subject of continuous research by many areas of business and industry. The advertising world conducts studies on color appeal to determine which colors sell packaged products, which colors attract the most attention on posters and on billboards, and which colors are most popular in automobiles. Color is big business in architectural design, interior decoration, and fashions. Unfortunately, people in general do not know very much about color. The consumer often makes costly mistakes in choosing the wrong colors in home furnishings that he will have to live with for years.

In the process of exploring the world of color, children will learn some basic color facts that will enable them to make the colors they want to use and to see how the colors act and interact on each other.

Crayon drawing, age 5½.

The way will open for children to develop intuitive feelings about color and to use it with imagination and discernment.

Color has three fundamental properties: HUE, VALUE, INTENSITY.

Hue is simply the name of the color — red, blue, yellow, green, orange, etc.

Value is the lightness or darkness of the color. The lighter colors are referred to as tints; darker colors, shades. Tempera paints may be made lighter by adding white; darker, by adding black. Transparent watercolors are lightened by adding clear water; shaded, by adding black. By using colors that are light in value with dark colors, contrast and interest can be achieved in painting. Such contrasts in painting help us to see form in painting. If everything in the picture were of the same value, it would be dull and monotonous.

Intensity is the brightness or dullness of a color. The brilliance of a color may be dulled or grayed by adding the complement of the color, for example, blue added to orange.

Some colors (red, orange, yellow) suggest warmth and have a tendency to advance or move out of the painted surface. Other colors (blue, green, purple) are often referred to as cool colors and tend to recede.

Red, yellow, and blue, colors that cannot be made by mixing other colors, are termed *primary* colors. Children should be encouraged to experiment with these colors, combining them in different ways to produce *secondary* colors (orange, green, purple) and other *intermediate* colors such as red-orange, blue-green, red-purple.

Show the children reproductions of paintings and prints, emphasizing how the artist used color to create feeling and mood, to visualize ideas; how the artist selected and used color to suit his own personal need — symbolically, quietly, explosively, daringly, inventively. Point out the effect when one color adjoins or overlaps another. What happens when colors of equal intensity or equal value are used in a painting? How can contrast, movement, and harmony be achieved through color?

Contrasting values of repeated shapes give a feeling of depth to this print by an eight-year-old child.

Section of a colored paper mural, a group project by seven-year-old children.

Texture

Texture, actual or represented, identifies surfaces as being smooth, rough, hard, soft, prickly, wet, dry. Texture is the way things feel to the touch or appear to the eye. An ice cube feels hard, cold and slippery; a rabbit, soft and furry; a tabletop, hard and smooth. Encourage the children to look around the school and in the community for interesting textures. There will be wood, metal, glass, cloth, brick, stone and perhaps an exhibit of rocks, shells, or coins. Rubbings may be made by placing a sheet of paper over a textured surface or object and rubbing over the reverse side with a soft pencil or crayon.

The painter often represents texture, visually, on the surface of his canvas or paper. A brass bowl may be painted to indicate a shiny smooth surface, reflecting the surrounding light; fabric to appear soft and silken. On the other hand, designers, craftsmen, architects, and sculptors express textural qualities in a direct way with the materials they use. An architect may use a combination of aluminum, limestone, wood, and glass in a way that he can accentuate their inherent textural characteristics as an integral part of his design. The potter may finish his clay bowl with a smooth, satiny surface or use a tool to produce unusual textured patterns in the clay.

Texture of tree bark.

Variety of textural patterns created in stitchery wall hanging by an eleven-year-old child.

Use of various textured items in child's interpretation of a figure, age 9.

Space

Artists concern themselves with two aspects of space — actual physical space and the two-dimensional, contrived space of the picture plane. The world's masterpieces of painting bear witness to the remarkable technological discoveries that artists have achieved in handling the problems of making space appear to be real. Through the elements of line, form, and color, the eye of the observer may be led into an illusion of three-dimensional depth as his eyes move

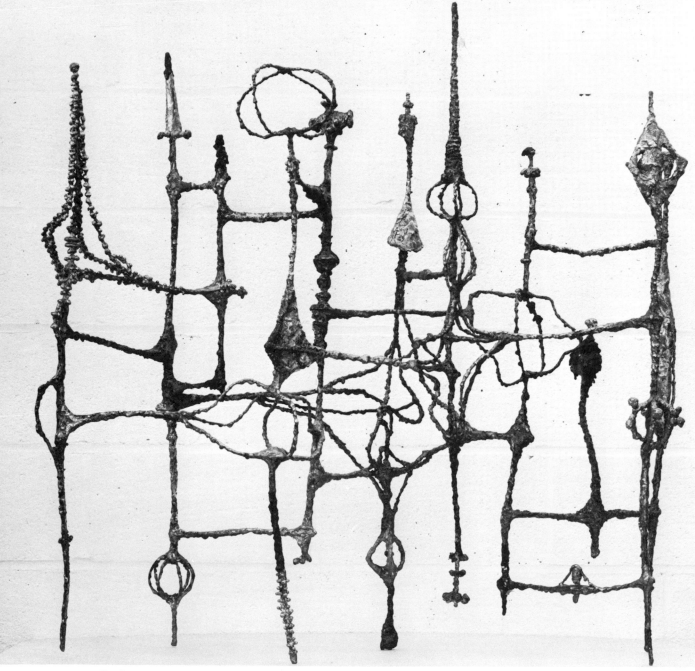

The Planets, various bronzes, by Ibram Lassaw. Courtesy Baltimore Museum of Art, Charles and Elsa Hutzler Memorial Fund.

in and around the objects in the painting. The discovery of perspective drawing gave the painter a device for expressing distance that sometimes seems to draw the vision to infinity. The overlapping of forms produces the feeling of distance between figures in the painting. The artist has discovered that empty space in a painting, sometimes called negative space because it has no objects in it, is as important to the total composition as the positive space. The shape, color, and value of negative space have much to do with the unity of the painting.

In the early 1920s the Bauhaus school in Germany developed new directions in the study of all aspects of design. Experiments in three-dimensional construction led to new concepts of space, especially in theatre design and architecture. The emphasis was on using materials of lighter weight to bring more space to interiors. The constructions of glass, metal, and other materials introduced new directions for sculpture which hitherto had been marble, stone, bronze, or wood. The mobile sculpture of Alexander Calder was a new space concept. Today it is a familiar art form.

Many young children get their first experience in space building through playing with blocks or using large cardboard cartons to make a playhouse. In order for them to grasp the broader implications of the importance of space in art, show them appropriate examples of painting, sculpture, architecture. Take space-walks into the school corridor, the cafeteria, outside. If possible, show them the relationship of empty space to buildings in a shopping center or the space between buildings in an urban renewal area.

Feeling of distance produced by interesting placement of trees in line composition, age 12.

Illusion of depth through size relationships of horse, wagon, and buildings in crayon drawing, age 7.

Overlapping and placement of figures create a feeling of depth. Tempera painting, age 10.

ACHIEVING
A SENSE OF DESIGN

Many products, mass-produced and used in the home, the community, offices, and schools, as well as those that are worn for comfort or personal adornment, are poorly designed and represent bad taste. Unfortunately, this is true, in many instances, of the graphic image projected by various communication media. Simply because something is designed, manufactured, and placed before the public is no guarantee that it is of good visual quality. One of the major purposes of teaching art to children is to

"Faun", stoneware, unglazed, by Frans Wildenhain. Photograph by Bill Giles. Courtesy American Craftsmen's Council, New York.

acquaint them with art products that are recognized for their excellence — to develop the child's visual and esthetic awareness and his ability to differentiate beauty from ugliness. Through seeing and association good taste can be cultivated.

How do artists, designers, craftsmen achieve a feeling of quality and a sense of organization in their work? Or create interest in communicating an idea with many different kinds of materials?

An understanding of the qualities (principles) of design will help children to answer these questions as they consider design in the environment, in the art of history, and in the making of their own paintings, prints, and three-dimensional designs.

The children's concepts of design qualities (unity, balance, rhythm, movement, variety) may be expanded and reinforced through SEEING good examples of art of the past and present, and through personal evaluation of their own art work. Through discussion they will become sensitive to the ways that painters used formal or informal balance for specific purposes; or how the architect accomplished an exciting variety in the design of a local building by the way he combined glass with stone and metal; or the manner in which the potter created a slow moving repeat pattern on the surface of a well-turned bowl.

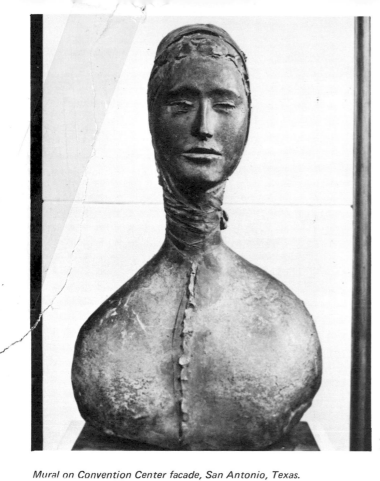

"Heffernan" Crest, sterling pin by Aniello G. Schettino. Photographer, Ed Del Fawa. Courtesy American Craftsmen's Council.

Bust da Inge by Giacomo Manzu. Southern Methodist University Collection.

Mural on Convention Center facade, San Antonio, Texas.

Unity

Unity is the harmonious organization of the component parts of a work of art into a single, complete, visually satisfying statement. Unity requires varying emphases so that there will be dominant and subordinate points in the design. The artist produces unity in many different ways, such as the repetition of a color, texture, line, or a shape in different parts of the design; the overlapping of objects or shapes; grouping of elements that form the design.

A sense of unity produced by repetition of shapes in architectural form. Palacio de los Deportes, XIX Olimpiada, Mexico.

Balance

Balance is the sense of visual equilibrium that is established in a work of art. This is accomplished by the artist in such a way that to move or eliminate any one part of the composition would disturb or "unbalance" the entire arrangement. Visualize a room with all of the furniture pushed to one side. This would give a feeling of being out of balance. Similar to this, a work of art, a painting, a sculpture with the heavy masses of form and color improperly distributed would appear to lack balance.

Building blocks and stacking objects, such as boxes, teach balance. Children also learn about balance on the playground seesaw or in riding a bicycle or when skating.

There are three basic types of balance that may be seen in paintings, sculpture, architecture.

Formal balance, also referred to as symmetrical balance, is based on an imaginary central line bisecting the design, resulting in one side of the design being an exact duplicate of the other side. This is the same idea as folding a piece of paper at the center and cutting a design that is the same on both sides when opened.

Show examples and discuss formal balance as it exists in nature and in man-made objects (shells, a turtle, the human figure, a primitive mask, a table, a chair, a vase, a building, an automobile viewed from the front). Does formal balance create a feeling of stability? dignity? restfulness?

Informal (asymmetrical) balance is the organizing of shapes or objects that are unequal in size or weight into an interesting, moving, balanced arrangement. The artist aims to achieve a "right" feeling of compositional weight or balance by the way he places objects that differ in size, shape, color, value, and texture in his design. For example, a large object placed close to the center of the painting may be balanced by a smaller object positioned farther from the center on the opposite side.

Medallion wall decoration by Olga Magnone;
Batik, tie-dye, and stitchery combined.
Courtesy American Craftsmen's Council, New York.

Radial balance is characterized in a design that radiates from a central point in a way similar to spokes on a wheel, petals on a flower, the crosscut section of an orange. Designs based on this type of balance, such as a rose window, are usually very decorative and appealing. They also have a very strong circular movement. Many primitive cultures have produced art that includes symbols of the sun with decorative rays around it. Young children frequently paint such symbols.

Computer art, an example of radial balance produced on a plotter system. Photograph courtesy California Computer Products, Inc.

Rhythm produced in scrap prints through repetition of single shapes.

Rhythm

Rhythm in art may be compared to rhythm in music; both project harmony and a feeling of movement. We hear the movement in music, we see it in painting, sculpture and architecture. When we dance or march or clap our hands to the beat of music, the very motion of our bodies accentuates our enjoyment of rhythm. An artist achieves the quality of rhythm by repeating shapes and colors and textures in a directional path which our eyes involuntarily follow as we look at the art work. In the observation and study of paintings it will be interesting to note the various ways that rhythmic movement has been accomplished.

Children who have many rhythmic experiences in school will soon be expressing a greater feeling of rhythm in their art products. The group repetition of rhyming verse as well as singing develops rhythmic feeling. The playing of soft rhythmic music in the room, as a background for art experiences, has proved to be an extremely inspiring rhythmic motivation.

Circular elements of an architectural tower project a rhythmic quality.

59

Movement

Works of the artist, designer, architect present varying tempos of movement from one point of interest to another in a composition. Without this quality the design would be quite static. The design may move the eye from the major point of interest to subordinate points or it may be the reverse, moving the eye throughout the arrangement in an orderly way to the center of interest. Movement in design is achieved by the repetition of shapes, colors, textures; through contrasting sizes of shapes; through the gradation of colors and values.

Drawing by a ten-year-old child. Movement reflects the roll of the sea through placement and repetition of boat shapes.

Variety

The artist develops a sense of variety in his art work to create interest, to give life to his ideas. Without variety there is monotony.

Variety is characterized in works of art by contrasting lines (size, type, direction), shapes, colors, and textures. Another way that the artist achieves variety is through the organization of different kinds of subject matter into his design.

Children enjoy variety and are easily drawn from one exciting adventure to another. This is often reflected in their painting, particularly through the many different colors that they use to express a single idea.

Stitchery wall hanging, age 11.

A growing sense of design

Achieving a sense of design is a desired by-product of the children's maturing concepts of the visual elements (line, form, color, texture, space) and the qualities of design (unity, balance, rhythm, movement, variety). Their growing awareness of design assists them toward a more meaningful understanding of the works of the artist; a greater sensitivity to design in the environment and of things; and a more satisfying experience in their own personal visual expression. They will talk about art and criticize ugliness.

Observe how children, when they are unhurried and undisturbed, stand back and evaluate their own work. Frequently, they will add shapes or color, change a line, or do something else to satisfy their appraisal of their work. This should be strongly encouraged. And time should be provided, free from pressure, so that this type of experience and personal evaluation may take place.

School bus, tempera paint, age 6.

Who can measure the personal satisfaction, the feeling of accomplishment, the delight that a young child enjoys through a personal art experience? Or the thrill that is his when he reshapes a paper bag to create a whimsical creature to perform at his command? Or the sense of fulfillment that he realizes when he proudly titles his latest masterpiece, "The

Big Black Pussycat"? The answer may be reflected in young eyes that see what adult eyes no longer see — or in the spontaneous enthusiasm that is characteristic of the uninhibited child.

For the young child, art materials and participation in art activities is primarily an opportunity for saying something — expressing an idea. It is a way of communicating an idea about his family, his brother or sister, or his dog, or a Sunday trip to the zoo. The young child, not yet influenced (hopefully) by adult standards, makes his visual statement through combinations of symbols and forms that are uniquely his. The process of handling materials, particularly those that allow free movement (paint or crayon on large sheets of paper), is in itself pleasurable to the young child.

Characteristic of the five or six year old is the enjoyment that he receives as he goes on an exciting

Tempera painting, age 5.

journey with paint or crayon across a piece of paper — leaving behind a maze of interlocking, varicolored lines — and shapes — amorphous, shapeless shapes. Enthusiastic and fascinated he reflects upon his personal, instinctive markings — symbolic of his own small world. Often incomprehensible to adults, this visual statement is tremendously important to the child — it is his! At this stage of the child's young life a new spirit is born — the spirit of discovery. In an atmosphere of acceptance and encouragement — a nod of approval, a few well-chosen words by an understanding teacher or parent — this early adventure in art will be climaxed with the child feeling a strong sense of achievement.

Unhampered by rigid rules and adult standards, the young child develops a natural control of and a personal application for art media as he gives outward expression to his inner feelings.

As the child grows, his expanding knowledge of self, of his environment; of art materials, tools, processes; of the visual elements and qualities associated with design, influence his creative work. Scribbles develop into more readily discernible symbols of his world — mother, father, baby sister, people, animals, objects around him. The development of smaller muscles enables him to achieve greater control over materials and expression. More detail appears in his art work.

The young child is an inventor — an imaginative inventor. He exaggerates the important (to him) and either avoids or eliminates that which is unimportant to his visual statement. A circle with two dots for eyes and a curved line for the mouth with legs and arms attached to the perimeter may be his visual representation of "mother". As other parts of the body become relevant he includes them.

Color at first is generally an emotional decision. It may be selected according to personal preference or may appear in the child's work simply because it was available. But the child's growing perception eventually assists him toward the relating of certain colors to particular elements in his picture: grass, trees, sky.

The young child is uninhibited. He enjoys working with art materials — producing new forms. He should be encouraged to express himself freely — to search and discover the potential of the art experience for him.

Tempera painting, age 6.

Painting, tissue paper and felt markers, age 7.

Chicken with rainbow tail, tempera paint, age 6.

Animal, construction, age 6.

Characteristics of the young child

There are distinct characteristics associated with this period of child growth that should serve as a basis for what may be anticipated insofar as visual expression is concerned:

• Short attention span at first developing in an ability to concentrate for longer periods of time and a capability for greater depth in visual expression.

• Development of small muscles coupled with greater eye-hand coordination and a capability for more intricate detail in art work.

• Symbolic representation of objects gradually changing to more interest in detail and a greater concern for realism.

• Inclination toward self-centeredness and independent activity at first, changing to a need for peer acceptance and an increasing interest in group relationships and activities.

• Spontaneous use of color at first, developing to a more specific and intentional concern for color to achieve realism.

• Little concern for actual size relationships of objects in a picture (emphasis on that which is important to him) to a developing understanding of true-to-life proportions.

• Space used to separate objects in a picture with no concern for depth or perspective, developing to early concepts of depth achieved by placing distant objects higher in the picture plane and later using the technique of overlapping.

Little Red Riding Hood, crayon, age 6.

• Earlier pleasures derived from manipulation of three-dimensional materials (clay, wood, boxes) lead to an inventive use of and a fascination with materials used in making puppets, masks, animals, figures, buildings.

• The younger child often produces what is commonly referred to as x-ray pictures. For example, he may draw an exterior view of a house and include himself watching TV inside of the same house. Or he may draw a picture of the school and on the reverse side of the paper show children eating in the school cafeteria. Paintings by the younger child are frequently characterized by a base line at the bottom on which he places objects and a strip of color at the top to represent the sky. As concepts of "horizon" develop, this feature disappears.

Tempera painting showing a natural feeling for design, age 6.

Expected behavioral changes

• The child grows in his capability for expressing feelings, observation, understandings, thoughts with various two- and three-dimensional art materials.

• The child increases in his dexterity with tools and materials.

• The child becomes more aware of his surroundings.

• The child becomes more secure in and achieves a sense of satisfaction through his personal visual expression.

• The child becomes more perceptive and observant through activities associated with the art experience.

• The child understands art terminology and elementary design concepts (color, texture, repeat, overlapping, space, form).

• The child becomes acquainted with and develops an understanding of the art of man.

Program of art experiences

The esthetic and creative growth of the child in the lower elementary school is manifested in different ways and at varying rates of development. Scribbles are followed by symbols and in turn replaced by a strong desire for representation. This generally parallels chronological, emotional, intellectual, and perceptive growth of the child. The art product of the child changes in form and content as his visual world expands, his muscle control develops, his concern for detail becomes more important; and as his discovery and understanding of the potential of art materials, tools and processes increases.

Under skillful guidance, the growing child will acquire a greater ability to observe, to sense, to organize thoughts, and to express personal ideas with two- and three-dimensional art materials.

This suggested program of art for the young child coordinates APPRECIATION, ENVIRONMENT, and ART ACTIVITIES at each grade level based on the interests and capabilities of the growing child. This is not a rigid format, but should be used with flexibility and adapted to specific school needs.

Tempera painting, age 6.

I. The World Of The Artist—
What is he saying?

The artist says many things through his art work. Often, he is telling us about something that he saw or experienced in his lifetime. Works of art that tell a story are particularly appealing to the young child. Thus, the choice of examples should be determined by the kind of subject matter that relates to the child's life experiences or falls within the realm of his somewhat limited understandings.

A suggested selection of paintings (reproductions) may include: *The Fifer* by Edouard Manet, *The Green Violinist* by Marc Chagall, *Signac and Friends Boating* by Pierre Bonnard, *The Three Umbrellas* by Raoul Dufy, *Backyards, Greenwich Village* by John Sloan, *The Peaceable Kingdom* by Edward Hicks. Examples of sculpture from ancient Egypt, often

Master Arthur (two circus figures), color aquatint by Georges Rouault. Nelson and Juanita Greif Gutman collection, the Baltimore Museum of Art, Baltimore, Maryland.

portraying the bird or animal form, interest this age level; also, selected pieces from primitive cultures. More recent works such as *Horse* by Edgar Degas and *Horse and Rider* by Mario Marini would appeal to the young mind.

It is not important that this early acquaintance with the art of man be encumbered with historical facts, such as dates, names, biographical sketches of artists. As a matter of fact, this approach should be avoided since it would have little meaning to the child.

Display the examples in a prominent place in the classroom and provide time for the children to LOOK, ENJOY, COMMENT, RAISE QUESTIONS. Discussion and interest may be stimulated through a few pertinent questions. What does the painting tell us? Is it a warm, happy story or is it sad? How does it make us feel?

This should be primarily a delightful, satisfying moment for the child that will ultimately lead to a desire for a more intense and knowledgeable relationship with works of art as he matures. On the plus side, initial concepts of color, shape and pattern may emerge naturally from this experience.

II. Our Environment—
Art and the home and the school.

In general, the world of the six-year-old child is relatively limited. The most important environment to him, prior to enrolling in school is that of his home and its immediate surroundings. This coupled with the contrasting space organization of the school and the route he travels between home and school should form the basis for any discussions or activities related to the nature of his environment.

Even here a rather simplistic, elementary approach should be adopted. The goal of this facet of the art program should be to open doors that will lead to a greater perception of and sensitivity to the natural and man-made things that exist in the home and school community.

One emphasis may be on the physical characteristics of the home and the school (man-made). What causes a room, a backyard, a playground to appear orderly and attractive? If a piece of trash is spotted on the floor, the sidewalk or the grass, should it merely be passed by? How does color on walls, furniture, floor coverings generate a certain feeling? Do pictures add interest? What kinds of pictures are on the walls at home? What would the children like to see on the

bulletin boards in the school? Ask the children to bring a favorite toy or book to school. Why do these have special appeal (color, shape, illustrations)?

Another focus may be placed on the natural elements of the school and home environment — trees, bushes, flowers, rocks, the sky above. Take the children on a SEEING walk in the vicinity of the school to examine more closely the natural environs. Talk about the various colors and shapes of things. How do each of these contribute to the general appearance of the environment? How does a huge, towering tree make one feel? How do the various colors observed and identified affect us?

Many points of interest will evolve from this experience. It is the beginning for forming design concepts, for opening young eyes to SEE things around them that are often missed — a crack in the sidewalk, a reflection in a puddle of water, a warm and friendly color; ultimately, this closer look at the immediate environment will assist the child toward attainment of discriminating and selective taste.

Tempera painting, age 6.

72

III. Creative Art Activities

Most children have had an opportunity to use some art materials prior to entering the first grade. It is not unusual for a three, four or five-year-old child to have made his mark at home with a crayon, pencil or even paints. Hopefully, the coloring book has not been a part of this preschool activity. But if it has been, avoid it now!

Insofar as materials and processes are concerned, there are a variety that are appropriate for beginning art experiences at this age level. These may include crayons, tempera paints, colored papers, clay, and different sizes and shapes of boxes for constructing activities; painting pictures, group murals, puppets and printmaking with scraps, objects and gadgets. It is not necessary for a child to engage in all of these activities. Some children may develop a strong interest in painting, achieving a real sense of satisfaction and pleasure in expressing ideas with large brushes and tempera paint. This should be encouraged. In general, however, most children will respond with characteristic childlike excitement and imagination to a varied program of two- and three-dimensional art activities.

This is not a time for emphasizing skills, techniques, and processes except as they grow out of the individual child's involvement with materials and personal expression. In advance of the time designated for art, organize adequate tools and materials and have them available to the children. Create an interesting classroom environment — bright colors, curious objects, lively bulletin boards. Encourage the spontaneous use of materials. Emphasize the spirit of the activity — the child telling his story visually, graphically, uniquely; searching the potential and discovering the characteristics of art materials. Assist the child, through discussion and listening, toward a specific and personal response to the art experience. What would he like to paint, model or construct? Make use of suitable motivational techniques such as dramatization, story-telling, demonstration, field trips. Experiencing art in this way will lead the child toward an awareness of design and a meaningful formulation of basic concepts. For example, primary colors (red, yellow, blue), warm colors, and cool colors relate effectively to his own symbolism. Talk about these ideas as they become a natural part of the child's experience.

Crayon drawing, age 6. Note typical base line.

Crayon rubbing and texture, age 6.

A. Drawing, painting

Tools and materials:

Wax crayons, tempera paint, finger paint, large sheets (12" x 18" and 18" x 24") of newsprint, manila or white drawing paper, colored construction paper, butcher paper, finger paint paper, want ad sections of newspapers, roll of 36" brown or white wrapping paper; ½" and ¾" bristle brushes, jars for water.

Emphases:

Discovering the characteristics of drawing and painting materials.

Expressing personal ideas.

Identifying primary colors.

Proper use and care of materials.

Activities:

Crayons

Provide the children large sheets of drawing paper (or newsprint). Conduct a "discovery" time. Suggest using broken pieces of crayon on the side; jabbing with the crayon (place a thick layer of newspaper under the drawing paper to serve as a pad) to produce dots and dashes of strong color; using several colors of crayon on want ad sections of newspapers; making crayon rubbings (place textured items such as cloth or wire mesh, corrugated board, cardboard shapes, leaves, string under the paper and rub crayons over the surface). Display and talk about the results of these experiments with crayon. What kinds of lines does the side of a crayon make? How do these differ from lines made with the point? How does the print on the want ad section of the paper affect the wiggly scribbly, thick, thin, criss-crossed, zig-zagged lines produced on it with various colors of crayons? Identify and name colors used. What happens when different colors are combined and overlapped? Does the amount of pressure or force used with a crayon affect the color produced? Plan color games in which the children guess the colors of objects around them.

"Searching" activities such as these will "free-up" the children — move them away from the tight, inhibiting use of materials. Working on large paper encourages a pleasant, swinging motion that is important to the development of muscular control and coordination.

Talk about ways in which these understandings may have application to the drawing of personal ideas with crayons (helping mother, a sunny day, my birthday, playing games, riding the school bus, my new dress).

There will be opportunity for the children to use many new media, but the crayon is a constant and ready tool for visual communication. Use it well. It assists the children in the development of their own self-image and this is extremely important.

Crayon drawing, age 6.

Witch, crayon, age 6.

Soldiers Marching, tempera painting, age 6.

Tempera paints

The classroom environment for tempera painting should be similar to that prepared for crayons — brightly colored bulletin boards, plenty of work space and materials ready for use. Sturdy cardboard boxes or shoe boxes may be used to hold several jars (baby food, jelly or small cans), each containing about one inch of paint (different colors) and a brush for each color. Jars for clear water should be available in addition to paint cloths and a stack of old newspapers to protect the floor. The paint should be a creamy consistency; the paper, large in size (white drawing paper, newsprint, colored construction paper, want ad sections of newspaper).

Whether working on the familiar two-sided easels or on the floor (covered with newspapers), the children will find this an exciting and exhilarating experience. Some of the children, using a large brush for the first time, will experiment, paint abstract shapes and symbols, drip paint, mingle colors on the paper; others will paint pictures of themselves, their family, their friends or of an impending holiday or event. The wide, long handled brushes and the free-flowing consistency of the tempera paint will combine to coax the most delightful paintings from the children. Few instructions from the teacher (other than care and use of materials) will be required. This should be a time of complete freedom for the children; the teacher assisting, commenting, suggesting, and praising as the need arises.

Display the completed paintings. Have the children talk about them. What colors can they identify? What happens when one color is mixed with another? How does painting with tempera paints differ from the use of crayons? What would happen if tempera paints and crayons were combined (crayons used over tempera paints after they have dried; crayon resist where slightly thinned tempera paint is brushed over a crayon drawing)?

Tempera painting, age 6.

Roller Skating, tempera painting, age 6.

Tempera painting, age 6.

Tempera painting, age 6.

Tempera painting, age 6.

Finger painting

Provide the children with large sheets of finger paint paper (butcher paper or freezer paper may be used). Wet the paper and smooth it rough side down, directly on the tabletop. Go over the glazed surface with a wet sponge. Place a spoonful of finger paint in the center of the paper. Encourage the children to use their fingers, flat part of the hand, edge of the hand and even forearms to move the paint into rhythmic swirls and designs. What happens when the fist, fingers or hands are used in a stamping action?

If the surface of the paint gets too dry, sprinkle a few drops of water on it. Finished paintings should be lifted by the corners and placed on open newspapers arranged around the edge of the room before this painting activity was started. Buckets of water, sponges and paper towels should be available for clean up.

Another type of classroom organization would be to designate a finger painting table where two or three children may work at a time while the rest of the class is engaged in another type of art activity.

If commercially prepared finger paint is not available, liquid starch may be smoothed rather thickly over the surface of the paper. Sprinkle colored tempera on top of this and proceed with the painting. The movement of the hands and fingers will blend the starch and tempera together.

An excellent motivation for finger painting designs is the use of music. As the children work, they pick up the beat and rhythm of the music and interpret it through their painting.

Display completed paintings. This will bring a natural flow of comments from the children. As in every art adventure, seeing, discussing and comparing the resultant products builds concepts and understandings of design and materials.

The mural

Group projects, such as murals, contribute to the child's ability to work with others, to make group decisions. At the same time, mural-making provides for the individual nature of the child, for each child adds his part to the total project.

Determine a theme, perhaps a carnival or festival to be held at the school; social studies are another good source for themes or topics. Through discussion the children should decide upon the elements to be included (clowns, booths, rides, costumes, balloons) and what part each child is to paint.

A long sheet of paper (rolls) may be stapled to cover the entire bulletin board. With materials organized, the children should take various stations and work directly on the paper. Another approach would be to give each child a large piece of paper on which to paint his part of the mural. The completed parts would be cut out and pasted in combination with each other on a long piece of paper. As the mural develops, the children may see the need for adding other things to it.

Mural, tempera paint.

Cutting and tearing

Another dimension for creating pictures is the cutting and tearing of paper (colored construction, newsprint, gift-wrap paper, colored magazine pages) and pasting the shapes to express an idea. Demonstrate and have the children experiment in tearing or cutting shapes. When using the printed page (magazine pages) point out that they are making new pictures of their own, utilizing the colors of the printed page. Some of the children may form complete figures or objects by tearing or cutting directly into the paper; others may combine and paste small torn pieces together on a sheet of plain paper to give shape to an animal.

Cutting with scissors may be a new experience for some of the children and plenty of opportunity should be provided for developing the skill. See that good scissors (not the dull blunt end type) are available for this activity.

As the skill in cutting and tearing increases and interest grows, the children may cut pictures that they have drawn or painted and re-combine them in various ways to make bulletin board displays and group murals.

Printmaking, age 6.

Scrap prints on display.

B. Printmaking with gadgets and things

Tools and materials:

Spools, corks, odd-shaped pieces of wood, mailing tubes, dowels, erasers, edge of cardboard scraps; tempera paint, bristle brushes; various colors of paper, newsprint, white drawing paper.

Emphases:

Discovering the printed image.

Searching the potential of ordinary objects (gadgets) as a means for personal expression and design.

Repeating a shape or unit to create interest in a design.

Activities:

The children may not be familiar with even the simplest of printmaking techniques but they have at one time or another gone through the process unknowingly (hand or finger marks on the wall, footprints in the sand or by placing bare feet in a puddle of water and walking across a sidewalk). Making a print with gadgets, unsophisticated as it may seem, will clarify the whole idea of creating an image by inking or painting a surface (gadget) and pressuring it against a piece of paper.

Make pads of newspapers to be placed under the paper to be printed. Have the children experiment with various objects suggested above. They may select one or more of the items available, paint the edge or surface with tempera paint (add liquid soap to the paint to retard drying) and stamp it against the paper. A variation would be to soak an ink pad with tempera paint, press the gadget against this and then print on the paper.

Talk about the shapes produced. Discuss color combinations; overlapping colors, colored tempera on colored papers. What is the effect when the print is made on the want ad section of a newspaper? What feeling is produced when one shape (gadget or object) is repeated? How can these designs be used (book covers, wrapping paper, place mats)? Observe and discuss the printed repeat design in things around the children (boys' shirts, girls' dresses, draperies at home).

An interesting follow-up experience would be to relate the printmaking process to a previous art activity, finger painting. Have a child place a piece of paper over a finger painting that is still wet, rub over this gently with a paper towel, pull up the paper and note the results. Two children should work together for this activity since it is necessary for one to have clean, dry hands to rub the paper on which the print is to be made.

Print made with pieces of sponge, cardboard tubes, other objects and tempera paint.

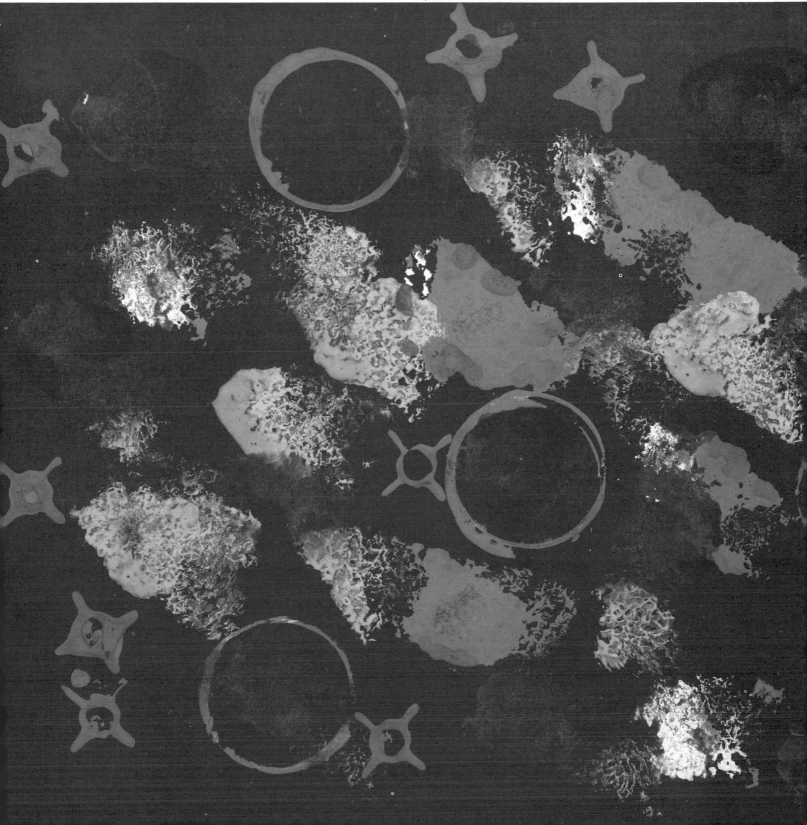

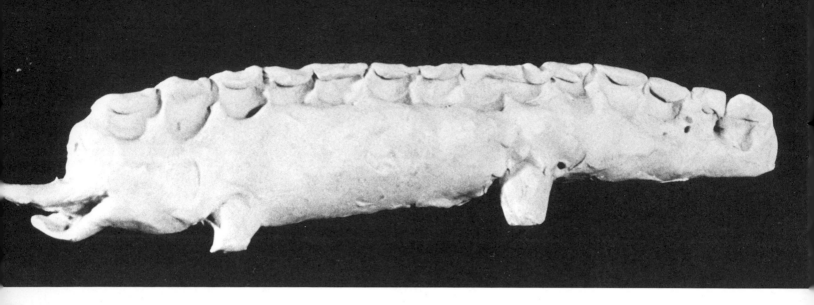

C. Modeling

Tools and materials:

Oil base clay; wet clay (pottery or ceramic clay); plastic bags; modeling boards (vinyl tiles, 12" x 12" wood or masonite shapes), texturing objects (paper clips, combs, bobby pins, buttons, nails, toothpicks, sticks).

Emphases:

Exploring the potential of plastic three-dimensional materials as a means for personal expression.

Building simple sturdy active forms.

Understanding texture.

Activities:

The soft, flexible, plastic qualities of various modeling materials have tremendous appeal to young children. Their past experiences in such manipulative activities probably include fascinating associations with mud forms and building mounds or castles in the wet sand at the beach.

Two kinds of materials are suggested for the school art program.

Oil base clay: a non-hardening clay that softens from the warmth of the hands.

Wet clay: There are many kinds of wet clay, dug from earth deposits, processed and mixed with water to a plastic consistency. Products made from wet clay may be fired and glazed to take a permanent form. Wet clay is generally available to schools in plastic bags, ready for use.

Each child should have a modeling board on which to work. Tables may be protected further with oil cloth.

Provide each child with a ball of wet clay. Suggest to the children that they just handle the clay to get the "feel" of it by pinching, pulling, rolling, stamping, poking, squeezing, cutting apart and rejoining. Have them flatten a lump of clay and texture a design into it with their fingertips or with some of the objects listed under "tools and materials".

Discuss the results of these exploratory activities. What does the clay suggest to the children? Would they like to make a figure or an animal? Have them experiment in pulling a three-dimensional form out of the ball of clay. Rather than add on legs or arms and a head, they should pinch and pull the clay to the shape they desire. These shapes may be somewhat crude, but they are very meaningful to the child.

As the children become more familiar with the clay and develop skill in handling, the forms will become more elaborate. Simple modeling tools and texturing objects may be used to refine and to develop additional interest in their designs.

Suggest a strong, bold, massive approach to design with clay. Avoid delicate parts that will crack and break off. Figures and animals should be constructed to stand alone.

When parts are added to a growing form, the clay must be scored and moistened at that point. If the clay gets too dry while using, add a little water. Cover clay work in progress with plastic bags to prevent hardening. When the clay objects are completed and thoroughly dry they may be fired in a ceramic kiln.

D. Building and constructing forms

Tools and materials:

Cardboard boxes of various sizes and shapes, mailing tubes, corrugated board, found objects, buttons, beads, corks, cans, dowels, string, rug yarn, raffia, tempera paints, colored paper, scotch tape, masking tape, brown gummed tape, staples, pins, wire, glue, brass fasteners.

Emphases:

Inventing new forms with common materials, discarded items.

Developing concepts of three-dimensional form.

Developing skill in the use of materials.

Activities:

Arrange a variety of the materials listed above on a table in the classroom for the children to discover. Provide opportunity for the children to handle the materials and ask questions. How can these materials be used to express or visualize an idea? What do they suggest? What can be made with them? Some of the boxes may relate quickly to specific things — a train, a rocket ship, an animal. Move some of the boxes around, creating different arrangements. Demonstrate techniques for joining — fitting, cutting, tying, taping, stapling.

A combination of cardboard tubes and boxes may eventually become an imaginative animal, a clown, a person. Cardboard tubes, used for a long neck, legs and arms, may be attached to a box by cutting a hole in the box and forcing the tube into it. Floppy ears, a tail, soulful eyes and other details should be added after the basic form has been constructed and painted.

A big cardboard carton may be transformed into a child-size automobile, a train, a house or something needed for a dramatic presentation or for a social studies unit. Encourage the children to explore the possibilities for converting a box to suit their plans. What is the box to be used for? If it is a house, what kind of roof should it have? How many windows? Will there be a garage? A yard? A dog house? A fence? Encourage the children to think and make decisions.

Materials such as these are quite stimulating to young children and many unique ideas will develop as the children work with them.

The Elephant's Trunk, construction, age 6.

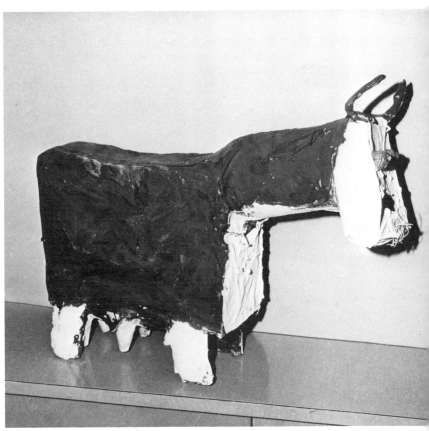

Cow, box construction, age 6.

E. Stick puppets
Tools and materials:

Sticks (12 to 18 inches long), staples, paper bags, cardboard or heavy paper, drawing and painting materials, decorative accessories.

Emphases:
Creating imaginative characters to interpret or dramatize a story.

Developing skill in the use of art materials.

Developing concepts of color, shape and personal expression.

Activities:
Making puppets is a natural and fascinating activity to satisfy the children's love for the dramatic. Any child who plays the part of a puppet grows in his ability to imagine, to perceive, to conceptualize and to create his own character to play a specific role. Puppet experiences assist the child in projecting himself and to speaking more clearly.

Stick puppet activities may grow out of a story, a song or a poem. Even at this age, however, the children may wish to prepare their own script, develop their own characters.

Stick puppets may be made by drawing or painting the characters on heavy paper or cardboard. These are cut out and stapled to the end of a stick. Yarn, buttons and other decorative items may be added. The puppets are now ready to perform. On with the show!

A variation would be to form the puppet head by stuffing a paper bag with shredded paper. Tie this to the end of a stick. How can this be decorated to create a specific character? Yarn for hair? Paints for the face? Buttons for eyes? The problems of construction are simple, the results — unlimited fun, learning, and entertainment.

Tempera painting, age 7.

I. THE WORLD OF THE ARTIST—
How does he say it?

While the artist uses his special skills to relate ideas, tell stories, record events, and to express his personal feelings through his art, he manipulates color and builds shapes that will best serve his purposes. Through selection and arrangement of color within a painting, for example, the artist can establish mood, determine points of interest and set up desired contrasts.

She-Goat, bronze by Pablo Picasso, 1950, collection The Museum of Modern Art, New York; Mrs. Simon Guggenheim Fund.

Reproductions (prints, filmstrips) should be selected on the basis of special appeal to the child. This may suggest, primarily, paintings, prints, and sculptures that are figurative, presenting familiar subject matter. However, works by such artists as Joan Miró (Large Composition) and Paul Klee (The Red Balloon) are very popular among young children. The highly personal, happy, childlike forms that are characteristic of Miró and Klee are colorful, exciting and fascinating.

Additional examples of art for study at this age level may include: *The Band* by Raoul Dufy, *Don Manuel* by Francisco Goya, *The Pineapple Vendor* by Diego Rivera, *Palomino Mother* by Millard Sheets, *The Marimba Players* by Phil Paradise, *The Boating Party* by Mary Cassatt, *Surfboatmen* by John Biggers, *The Gulf Stream* by Winslow Homer. Also, sculptures: *Indian Hunter* by Paul Manship, *Buffalo Horse* by Frederic Remington and examples of Pre-Columbian art (Maya, Aztec, Inca cultures).

Display a selection (3 to 5 examples) of reproductions in the classroom where they may be easily seen. Provide time for the children just to SEE and ENJOY. Then talk about the paintings or sculptures. How has the artist used color to create mood? Name the dominant colors. How do these contrast with other colors in the painting? In what way does the use of color give life to the painting? Ask the children if they would select other colors to tell the same story. Discuss the shapes used by the artist. What kind of a feeling do they project? Is there a sense of movement in the piece of art? What point first attracts the eye? Where does the eye move from here? Who is the artist? What was it like at the time he lived?

Second in importance to enjoying the works of art is that the children understand some simplified concepts of color, contrast, shape and movement; how the artist organized these elements to express an idea; how the children will be concerned with the same factors in their own work. Also, this should be the starting point for relating a piece of art to a specific artist or period of time.

Busto di Giovane, bronze by Arturo Martini, collection Southern Methodist University, Texas.

The paramount goal of this focus on environmental experiences of the children is to help them SEE the world around them. Although children are naturally curious, they (like adults) often move about without really SEEING the physical and natural world which is a part of them. By developing a closer understanding of the elements which give shape to the local environment — what they are, why they exist — bases may be established to assist the child toward becoming more concerned about the condition of his community; toward the acquiring of discriminating taste; toward a greater esthetic awareness.

What is the physical nature of the community? How does one part differ from another (residential, business, industry, commercial, recreation)? Why? What do the children see on their way to school? Have the children name as many things as possible. Which of these are natural objects; which, man-made?

There are a variety of art projects related to environmental awareness that should follow-up this LOOK at the community. Have the children draw or paint from memory, scenes based on the local community. Involve them in designing a bulletin board ("A Litter-Free Community", "Landmarks in Our Town", "Paintings of Our Neighborhood"). The interest of the class may even lead to the painting of a mural based on the environment.

II. OUR ENVIRONMENT— The neighborhood (space between home and school)

As the child grows the horizons of his world broaden and the boundaries of his experiences expand. While earlier environmental observations were directed primarily to the home and school, at this age level the emphasis may be a closer LOOK at the local community — more specifically the variety of spaces through which the child travels for one reason or another. These may include his route to school, the space between home and the shopping center or downtown, the church, the home of a friend or relative.

Freeway and skyline, Houston, Texas. Texas Highway Department photograph.

Judy

Cowboy, tempera painting, age 7.

III. CREATIVE ART ACTIVITIES

The art program at this age level should expand upon the understandings, concepts and skills developed through previous art experiences. Many of the art activities will be more or less familiar to the children but new materials and new emphases should assist them toward a broader understanding of design and a greater sense of satisfaction and enjoyment as they adapt various art processes to their own personal visual expression.

The natural curiosity of the child should be encouraged in his use of materials as he seeks for himself their potential, becomes familiar with their characteristics and develops control and skill in handling them.

Bear, ceramic, age 7.

A. Drawing and painting

Tools and materials:

Wax crayons, tempera paint, finger paint, large sheets (12″ x 18″ and 18″ x 24″) of newsprint, manila or white drawing paper, colored construction paper, butcher paper, finger paint paper, classified section of newspapers, roll of 36″ brown or white wrapping paper, ½″ and ¾″ bristle brushes, jars for water.

Emphases:

Understanding various ways to use crayons; tempera paints.

Identifying secondary colors (orange, green, purple); light and dark colors (value).

Developing concepts of texture, form; variety of line and shape relationships.

"Girls Like To Play Mother", crayon, age 7.

Activities:
Crayons

Talk about experiences familiar to the children. What do they see on the way to school? How do they travel to school? By bus? Bicycle? Walking? What do they see: neighbors, boys and girls, policemen, houses, stores, dogs and cats, cars, trucks, things growing, sidewalks, streets, freeways? List on the chalkboard. Encourage the children to visualize what they are going to draw — to close their eyes and see one thing to draw. Suggest using the whole sheet of paper. Make suggestions as needed. Compliment the children on their good ideas and use of the crayon.

Talk about ways the crayon may be used to make pictures more expressive. How can small broken pieces be used to dot and jab to create areas of texture? What happens when one color is rubbed on top of another? How can crayons be used to produce different values of color (light and dark)? Demonstrate as the need arises.

Arrange to have an animal (dog, cat, rabbit, hamster) in the classroom for the children to observe and draw. The lesson may be organized to include painting. Some children may wish to model the animal in clay. Discussion of the results should emphasize the variety that may be achieved with different kinds of art materials.

Ask one of the children to pose so that the rest of the class can draw him (her). Focus attention on how the body bends or moves at the waist, knees, shoulders, neck, elbows. Have the model bend, twist, jump and run while the class observes. Discuss the action. Where do the hands reach when the arms are dropped straight down? Are the eyes in the middle of the head? What is the location of the nose and mouth? Are all of the children the same height? Experiences and observations such as these assist in developing a "readiness" for drawing the figure. Pose the "model" holding a baseball bat or lifting something. Avoid hackneyed drawing formulae (stick figures, sausage shapes, egg heads). Talk about expression, action, and the general appearance of the figure.

Have the children explore the possibilities of *crayon rubbings.* This technique is one in which the paper is placed on top of textured materials or a textured surface and the side of a crayon is rubbed over the surface until an image appears. Leaves and tall wild grasses or weeds make exciting rubbings. Introduce other textured materials (chicken wire, mesh, corrugated cardboard, netting) and suggest the use of several colors of crayon on the same rubbing.

Figure drawing, crayon, age 7.

Cut cardboard or heavy paper shapes, arranged under a sheet of paper and rubbed with crayon, will be effective in developing concepts of shape and the relationship of different shapes to create interest.

Discuss ways in which the technique of crayon rubbing may be used in drawing pictures.

Crayon rubbing. Single cut cardboard figure placed in different positions under paper and crayon rubbed over surface, age 7.

Crayon rubbing, leaves, age 7.

"Watching the Seals", tempera painting, age 7.

Tempera paint

Organize the classroom so that tools, materials and work spaces are ready. If dry tempera paint is to be used, mix approximately nine tablespoons of the powdered pigment with three cups of water in a jar and shake well. The paint should be a creamy thickness. Prepare several sets of paint for the children (baby food jars, each containing about one inch of a color; sturdy cardboard carton to hold jars; bristle brush for each color). The tables may be moved into painting clusters or moved out of the way so that children can sit or kneel on the floor to paint. Have plenty of newspapers ready to protect working surfaces; clean water and sponges for clean-up.

Motivation for painting should be similar to that for drawing activities — experiences of the child, figures,

animals. Talk about painting single objects that may be cut out later and arranged on the bulletin board. Suggest that the children paint themselves in an imaginary situation.

Discuss the mixing of colors. What happens when red and yellow are mixed? Blue and red? Yellow and blue? What happens when white or black is added to a color? Have the children use primary (red, yellow, blue) colors to produce other colors. Leak-proof, plastic egg cartons are ideal for this activity. Suggest painting with these colors on the classified ad section of the newspaper. Encourage the children to exchange colors.

Introduce other tools for painting. One interesting item that will add textural qualities to painting is the cellulose sponge. What will result when a sponge is

Tempera painting from the Children's and Young People's Classes, the Art Center, The Museum of Modern Art, New York.

dipped into tempera paint (quantity of paint poured into an aluminum pie pan) and then pressed against the paper? Have the children experiment. What other things could be used?

At this age level, the children's paintings will begin to reflect a more highly developed composition; objects appearing on more than one base line; greater awareness of details. Display and discuss their painting. Recognition, praise and encouragement are powerful motivating factors.

An extension of individual picture painting is the *mural*. Staple a long strip of paper (bright color if available) on the bulletin board. Talk about murals and their purpose as wall decorations, depicting a story. Discuss themes and organize the class for designing and painting the mural. How does the bright colored paper relate? Would the children like to paint directly on the long strip of paper or paint individual parts to be cut out and pasted to it? The mural is quite effective when developed in relation to other areas of the school program. It promotes learning and results in a greater retention of the things learned.

Tempera painting based on Columbus Day theme, age 7.

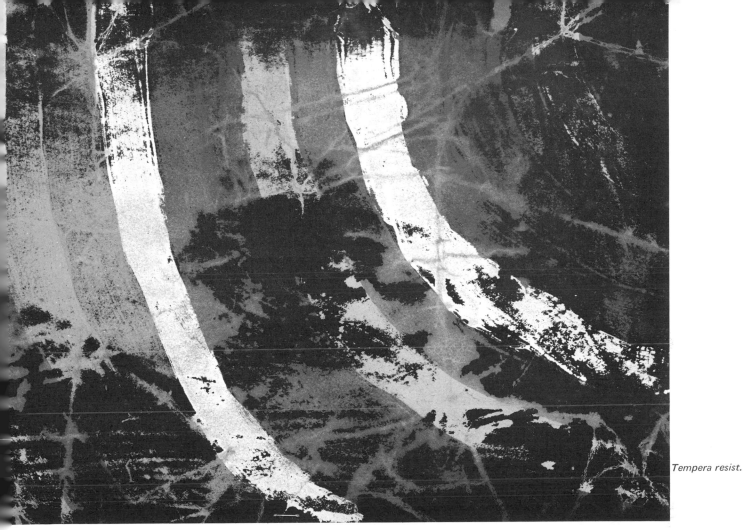

Tempera resist.

Mural, group project, age 7. Theme, Jungle Animals. Colored tissue paper and felt markers.

Finger paint

Finger paint paper (butcher or freezer paper) should be thoroughly dampened in clear water, smoothed with rough side down on the tabletop and wet again with a sponge and clear water. A tablespoonful of finger paint placed in the middle of the paper, spread over the surface with the hand will soon be transformed into whirling, rhythmical, sparkling designs by the dancing fingers of young children.

Play a recording with a rhythmic beat that will have special appeal to the children. Encourage the children to sway body and arms to the music. Ask them to describe the way the music makes them feel. If the paint gets too dry, add several drops of water.

Finger paints may be combined with crayons. Have the children make rhythm pictures using wax crayons on dry finger paint paper. Then follow the same finger paint procedure described above.

Design, finger paints combined with crayon, age 7.

Finger painting, age 7.

Cut paper design, age 7.

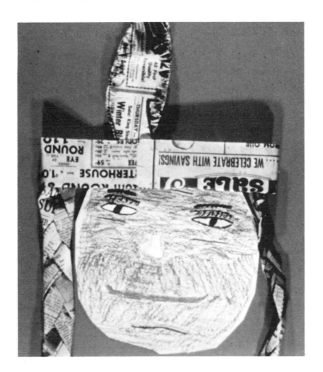

B. Cutting and tearing

Tools and materials:

Drawing paper, colored construction paper, colored tissue, newspapers, magazine pages, gift wrapping paper, thin cardboard, corrugated cardboard, paste, glue, tape, liquid starch, felt markers, tempera paint, scissors, brushes.

Emphases:

Understanding various techniques for cutting and shaping paper.

Developing three-dimensional qualities in picture-making.

Activities:

What can be done with paper other than using it flat for drawing and painting? Some of the children will recall that during a previous art activity they formed pictures by cutting and tearing shapes and pasting them on a sheet of paper.

Provide the children with strips of paper, an inch or so wide. Have them practice folding, pleating, twisting, curling, fringing. Demonstrate when necess-

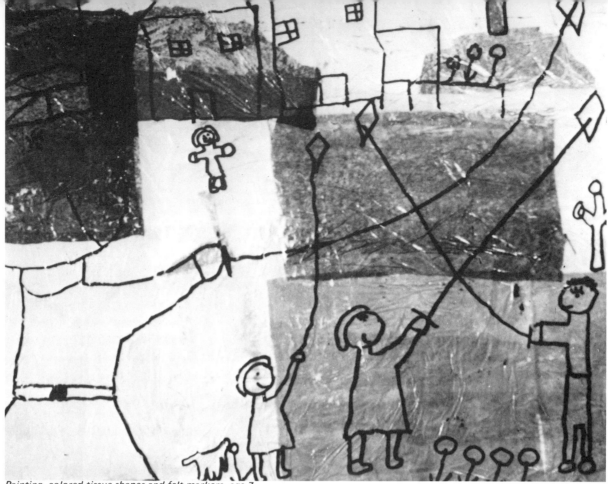

Painting, colored tissue shapes and felt markers, age 7.

ary. What happens to the paper when it is wrapped tightly around a pencil and then removed? Fold a wider piece of paper in half and make narrow scissor cuts along one side to the middle of the fold. What happens when this fringed part of the paper is pulled between the thumb and a pencil? How can these techniques be used in making a three-dimensional picture or design?

Understanding of form in designing with paper may be developed through the designing of one-fold animals. The technique is simple and the opportunity for imaginative results is great. Have the students fold a piece of colored paper in half, stand it on the desk with the folded edge up and observe. How can this be changed to create an imaginary animal? What can be added to it to add interest? Do the folding, curling, fringing techniques have application? Unusual color combinations should be encouraged.

Another combination of materials would be colored tissue and felt pens on large sheets of white drawing paper. Follow the same motivation used in other drawing and painting activities. However, in this experience the drawing would be simply with lines made with a felt marker on drawing paper. Color may be introduced by arranging shapes of colored tissue over the drawing and brushing a light coat of liquid starch over this. What happens where the colored tissue overlaps? Another approach would be to cut the drawing apart and add colored tissue to individual parts. Then prepare a background sheet by arranging varied colored shapes of colored tissue over a sheet of paper and brushing with liquid starch. After the starch has dried, arrange the formerly prepared parts and paste in position. Then add another thin coat of starch. How can felt pens be used to add details? To give emphasis?

These same techniques may be used in making a mural. Follow organizational procedures for mural making as described earlier. Then apply the techniques for using colored tissue and liquid starch to making the individual parts of the mural. Other materials may be used in the completion of the mural to add interest, emphasis and unity. For example, rug yarn may be glued onto certain sections of the mural to produce strong linear and textural qualities.

C. Wet clay and pinch pots

Tools and materials:

Wet pottery clay, simple texturing tools (combs, nails, toothpicks, paper clips), tongue depressors, rolling pin, several sticks ¼" x 1" x 12", modeling boards (12" x 12" pieces of vinyl or masonite), protective covering for tables (oilcloth, plastic bags from the cleaners).

Emphases:

Understanding three-dimensional form.

Becoming familiar with the characteristics of clay and simple techniques for modeling.

Developing concepts of texture.

Activities:

Careful preparation for clay modeling activities would include covering work spaces with oilcloth or plastic, providing individual modeling boards for each child, and arranging buckets, water and sponges for efficient clean-up. Each child should have at least one ball of clay about the size of an orange.

While the children are handling the ball of clay discuss some of its characteristics. How does it feel? What can be done with it? Using the ball as a basic

Pinch pots combined.

form, suggest pressing it firmly on the modeling board. What happens? Does this look like anything? If both thumbs were pressed down into the center of the clay, how would this change its appearance further? Does this have any possibilities as a container or pot? Encourage the children to continue, pressing the inside gently to expand the size and roundness of the pot (pinch pot). Wet the fingers and smooth the inside. Be careful not to get it too wet. Stop and look at the object at this point. What are some of the things that can be done to it to complete it? Talk about smoothing the top edge or pinching it to make a simple design; using a texturing tool to create a design on the outer surface of the pot; smoothing the outer surface with wet fingers; pressing small balls of clay on the outer surface to form another type of design. The clay pots may be left to dry and then be fired and glazed. On the other hand, the clay may be rolled into a ball again. Press a shallow hole in the ball, fill with water and stack the balls carefully in a covered crock or plastic container, for future use. The small amount of water seeps into the clay and keeps it in good, workable condition.

Left on their own, children naturally model the most exciting little figures of people, animals and the world of fantasy. Encourage such activity. Displaying and talking about their clay pieces increases the children's

vocabulary and often reveals new insights that help the teacher to work more understandingly with the children.

Another direction for clay activities would be to have the children flatten a ball of clay on the modeling board, place a stick 1/4" x 1" x 12" on each side and roll a rolling pin across creating a smooth flat slab, 1/4" thick. A paring knife may be used to cut a tile, 3" x 4", 4" x 4" or some other desirable size. What can be done with this? Perhaps a design can be drawn on the surface with a nail or a stick. Could a design be made by pressing something into the clay? Try an interesting found object, a gear, a shape of wood, the end of a dowel. How could the finished product be used? It may be attractive as a wall tile. If so, before firing and glazing, be sure to pierce a hole in the appropriate place so it can be hung.

103

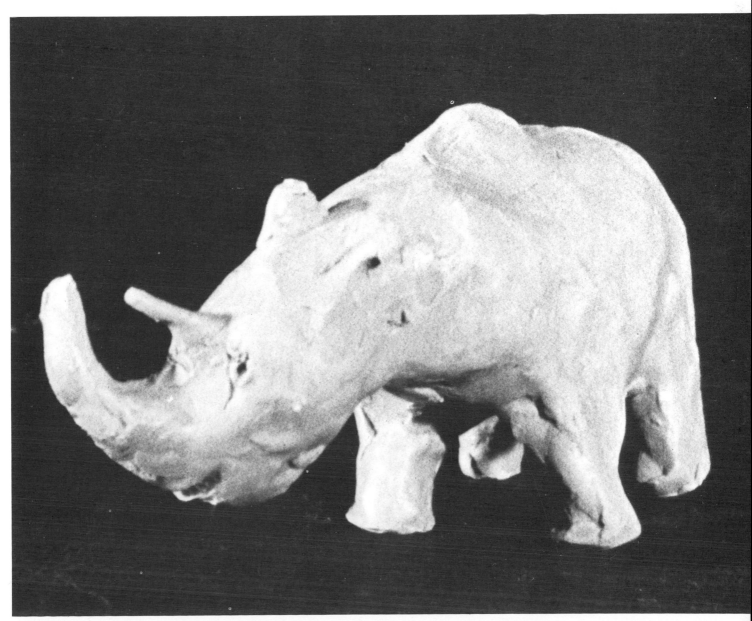

D. Casting and sculpture

Tools and materials:
Beach sand, pebbles, shells, found objects, wood scraps, molding plaster, cardboard shoe boxes and gift boxes, plastic bowl.

Emphases:
Understanding a simple casting technique.

Developing concepts of three-dimensional form (relief sculpture).

Activities:

The process of sandcasting is relatively simple, yet fascinating to children and adults alike. It is certainly within the realm of capability for the average seven-year-old child.

Although this is suggested here as a classroom activity, if a sandy beach is available, the excitement can be multiplied many times.

Since this is a different type of art experience than the children have had, it may be best to start with a demonstration. This should be planned to show the procedure and to open up design possibilities. Involve some of the children in the demonstration.

Place about two inches of damp sand in a sturdy box. Smooth the surface. Ask one of the children to press his finger or hand into the sand. What happens? Another child should be invited to press an object into the sand. Ask him to remove the object and describe the result. After several such impressions have been made in the surface of the sand discuss the procedure for making a cast of the resultant "design". Mix molding plaster by sifting it into a plastic container holding clear water. Have one of the children stir the mixture with a stick. When the plaster gets as thick as cream, ask another child to pour it slowly over the sand design until it reaches a thickness of approximately one inch. This should remain in the box for about one hour. Clean the bowl by scraping the remaining plaster onto newspaper. Keep plaster away from the sink since it would harden in the pipes and clog the drain.

When the plaster casting is thoroughly dry and hardened, remove it from the box. Brush off loose sand but leave that which is firmly adhered to the plaster. Discuss the results. Note that the plaster cast is actually the opposite of the impression in the sand. What does this indicate? The children should conclude that the holes, wells or impressions in the sand are now raised parts of the design. Discuss other ways in which designs may be formed and cast in sand. In addition to pressing forms or objects in the sand to create the design, could pebbles be arranged on the surface and become a part of the plaster? Shells? Other objects? Encourage the children to experiment.

If the sandcasting is to be displayed by hanging on the wall, insert paper clips or loops of wire in the back before the plaster sets. Wire may be attached to these later for purposes of hanging.

E. Three-dimensional design and the bulletin board

Tools and materials:

Colored construction paper, newspaper, kraft paper, small boxes and cardboard tubes, long straight pins, tempera paint, brushes.

Emphases:

Relating visual expression to other areas of the school program; to world events.

Developing concepts of three-dimensional (sculptural) form.

Participating in a group project.

Activity:

The bulletin board itself is an excellent and inviting design surface. Accustomed to working with various art materials distributed to them for individual projects, the children will find the large surface of the bulletin board an interesting challenge for a group design project.

Motivation should be similar to that used for group mural activities. Themes may be derived from social studies, reading, science, world events, health, environmental concerns.

A major emphasis of this experience is to broaden the children's concepts of three-dimensional design. What does "three-dimensional" mean? How does this contrast with the flat surface of a sheet of paper? The flat surface of the bulletin board? What examples of three-dimensional form can be found around us?

Examine the materials that have been organized for this art project (various sizes of boxes, cardboard tubes). How do these relate to the theme selected for the design? What can the children do with these materials to transform them into figures, animals, cars, airplanes, rockets? Determine the various components of the bulletin board construction and proceed. As the different parts are constructed discuss the possibilities of color to be used in completing them. What may be added to enhance these objects? Discuss the background colors and shapes to be used on the bulletin board.

Talk about arrangement of the individual parts to create unity, movement and interest in the design. The constructed objects may be attached to the bulletin board with long straight pins (bankers' pins). A stapler may also be used.

What should the caption for this display be? Suggest lettering with bristle brushes and tempera paint on the classified ad section of the newspaper. This lettering technique is described on the following pages.

F. Lettering words and titles

Tools and materials:

Flat bristle brushes (1/2" or 3/4"), tempera paint, classified ad section of the newspaper, scissors, paste, pins.

Emphases:

Developing understanding of the letter form.

Providing experience in lettering with a bristle brush.

Activity:

Lettering is a highly skilled form of visual expression. Much practice is necessary to become proficient in the handling of various tools and materials associated with lettering.

At this age the concern should not be so much for skill as it should be for providing experience and utilizing simple techniques that will build confidence and assure success.

Most seven-year-old children are familiar with the printed alphabet. They are accustomed to using ruled paper (guide lines) and soft pencils or ball-point pens to letter words, numbers and sentences; and take great pride in their ability to form letters and numbers with these tools. Unfortunately, this skill is frequently forgotten when the children are taught cursive writing. Teachers of upper grade children are often dismayed at their inability to letter a caption for a display or their name on a portfolio. Teachers of young children can do much to help them retain their ability to letter by giving them simple and frequent lettering experiences that will develop skills.

Display examples of gothic lettering on the bulletin board. Discuss the characteristics of the letters. What are their similarities? How do they differ? Gothic letters are all the same thickness, formed with straight lines, curved lines, combinations of both. Provide the children with classified ad sections of the newspaper, brushes and tempera paint. Turning the paper sideways and using the lines dividing columns as guide lines, suggest making straight lines, curved lines, "S" lines. Demonstrate the combination of straight lines to make the A, E, F, H, I, K, L, M, N, T, V, W, X, Y, Z. Encourage the children to make these letters; to get the feel of the brush. Have them practice brushing the other letters and then combining to form words. Talk about the results. How can these letters be used? Could they be cut out and pinned or stapled to the bulletin board to form a caption.

Most children will be pleased with their accomplishments, particularly if a little praise is offered. Since continuing practice and practical application is important to building lettering skills, provide a corner in the room with paper, paint and brushes where children may pursue their lettering interests at various times throughout the day. They will take pride in lettering their names, titles for bulletin boards and showcases and simple signs for the school.

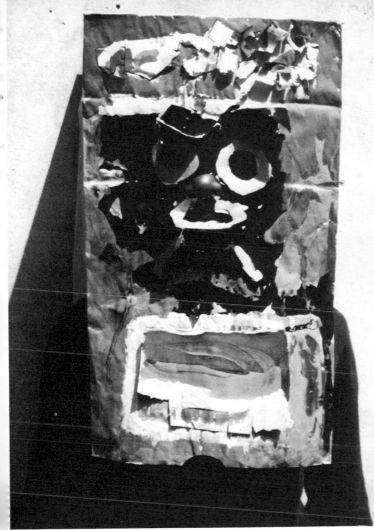

Paper bag mask, age 7.

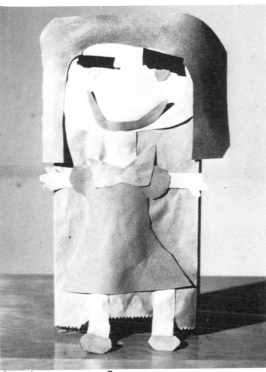

Paper bag puppet, age 7.

G. Masks, puppets and imagination

Designing masks and creating puppets is a delightful activity for children at all ages. Such experiences have tremendous appeal to the children making masks and puppets as well as those who will be enjoying the ultimate dramatic presentation. This activity also has significant value in the promoting of favorable group attitudes and the developing of speech, personality and imaginative qualities of the children.

Mask and puppet projects should involve the children in writing their own script, determining the characters, designing and constructing scenery and, finally, — the dramatic presentation.

Motivation may be the designing and making itself, with the story evolving from the experience. On the other hand an interesting story, poem, song or experience of the children may serve as a starting point for this adventure into the world of fantasy and dramatics.

Mask and puppet making is much more than merely decorating paper bags. Show examples of primitive masks and Indian totems to the children. Discuss the qualities that make these examples interesting — design, shape, color, action, the feeling that they give. What is the mood represented in the designs? Happy? Sad? Angry?

What kind of mood will the children want to project through their masks or puppets? How can this be achieved? Discuss methods of construction, techniques for decorating and materials that will best assist in the interpreting of an idea.

Paper bag masks

Tools and materials:

Paper bags large enough to fit over the children's heads, colored paper, tempera paints, an assortment of decorative materials (yarn, raffia, beads), scissors, paste.

Paper bag puppet, age 7.

Activity:

The paper bag may be fitted over the child's head so that he can determine the location of the eyes, nose, mouth. Holes should be cut through the bag (after it has been removed) for the eyes and, if desired, for the nose and mouth. Place the bag flat on the table while completing the design. When the general design of the mask is completed, open the bag and stand it up for evaluation. What may be added to create more interest? Yarn or raffia for hair? A small box for the nose? Large paper ears?

Paper bag puppets

Tools and materials:

Small paper bags, tempera paints, brushes, colored construction paper, string, paste.

Activity:

The bag should be folded as it was when it was new, with the bottom flat to form a rectangle. Have the children experiment with this by slipping their hand into the bag and manipulating. Does this action suggest the movement of a mouth? Where would the eyes and nose of the puppet be placed? Try cutting the teeth and tongue out of colored paper and pasting them in the mouth opening. What materials can be used to complete the puppet? Paint or paper for the eyes? In what ways can yarn, cloth, ribbon and buttons be used to make the puppet more interesting and expressive? Place the finished puppets over coffee cans for display purposes. Plan a puppet show. Make a stage with the necessary scenery. Invite another class in, and — on with the show!

Paper bag puppet made by stuffing the end of the bag with newspaper and tying, allowing hole in the neck for the finger; cloth dress and decorations added.

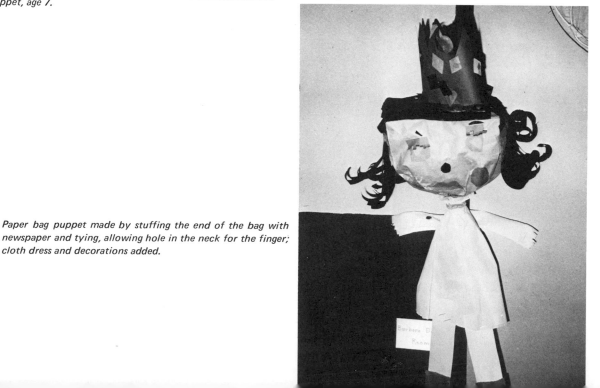

H. Cardboard and a print

Tools and materials:
Thin cardboard, bookbinders board, newspapers, colored construction paper, tempera paint (or water base printing inks), brushes, yarn, string, cardboard tubes, brayers, scissors, ink slabs (vinyl squares).

Emphases:
Broadening concepts of printmaking through a rather simple technique.

Discovering line, shape, color and pattern in printmaking.

Activities:
Printmaking is the process of duplicating images or designs by applying ink to a specially prepared "block" and pressuring it against a piece of paper or some other kind of material. Many images (impressions) can be produced from the same block. A variety of results may be achieved by overlapping the prints, by changing color combinations of ink and paper and by printing on different kinds of backgrounds (paper on which colored tissue shapes have been glued; paper over which a brayer has been rolled producing shapes of color). Encourage the children to experiment.

Discuss the preparation of a cardboard printing block: cutting rectangles, free shapes, people, animals, buildings from cardboard; arranging these shapes to form a design; gluing the shapes on another piece of cardboard (bookbinders board). The block is now ready.

Organize the room for making the prints. Tempera paints and brushes (or inking plates, brayers and water-base printing inks) should be set up in stations to provide easy access. Several thicknesses of old newspaper should be available to make soft pads under the paper being printed. Have one of the children demonstrate for the class by brushing (or rolling) tempera paint (or inks) over the cardboard printing block. Press the block against a piece of paper. Discuss the results. Repeat this by making a series of prints on the same piece of paper. What other shapes can be used in combination with the block? Try the edge of a piece of corrugated cardboard, a cork, a piece of sponge. Talk about the results. Why does the block print a specific design? Could other materials be used in the making of the printing block to achieve different results? Try gluing string or yarn to a cardboard shape to make a printing

block (also, toothpicks, paper clips, rubber bands, felt shapes).

Provide opportunity for the children to experiment with brayers for printmaking (cardboard tubes may be used). Suggest wrapping string around the brayer, inking it by rolling across an ink slab (a rectangular foil pan containing several layers of soft cotton cloth, dampened with water and coated with tempera paint will serve the purpose) and then rolling across a sheet of paper. Let this dry and, using a contrasting color, roll the brayer across the first design.

Combine the brayer printing with cardboard printing.

Printmaking offers many possibilities for invention. Through this experience, the children will become sensitive to changing patterns that emerge and interesting color combinations.

Print made with cardboard tubing over paper shapes.

110

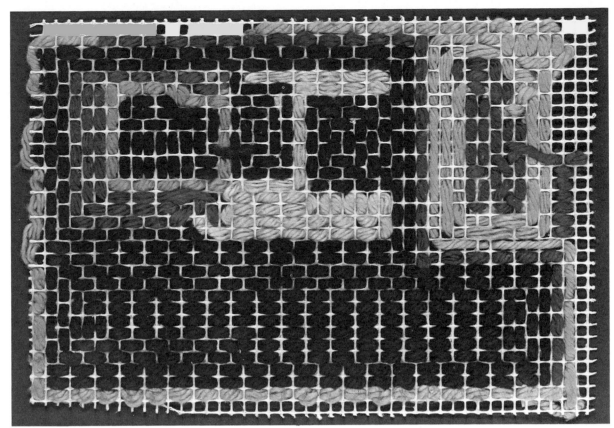

Weaving on mesh, age 7.

I. Textiles and design

Tools and materials:

Wire, plastic or cloth mesh, mesh vegetable and fruit bags, rug yarn, ribbons, string and lacings, masking tape, large darning needles, bobby pins, scissors.

Emphases:

Broadening concepts of texture, color and pattern.

Developing skills in weaving on mesh.

Activities:

Discuss the weaving process. Show examples of weaving on mesh. Talk about design and how interest in color and texture may be achieved with a variety of materials. Provide the children with rectangles of mesh cut from vegetable or fruit bags. Demonstrate by weaving a length of yarn, in and out of a row of the openings in the mesh. This demonstration should include the cutting of yarn to an appropriate length, the tying of the yarn (not in a knot) to the loop of a bobby pin, weaving the yarn in the mesh and finishing the length of yarn by pulling the end to the underside of the weaving. Also, demonstrate the starting of another strand of yarn by leaving an inch or more hanging loose on the back of the weaving. Experiment with combining different yarns and ribbons.

Weaving on mesh, age 7.

As the children work on their own designs they will need guidance toward keeping the yarns loose to prevent bunching and puckering of the mesh.

Encourage experimentation — free form shapes, open areas, adding of unusual materials.

Weaving on wire, plastic or cloth mesh may be somewhat easier because the mesh is generally stiff. Bind the edge of wire mesh with masking tape to protect hands and fingers.

After the children learn the basic process of weaving on mesh they will be interested in exploring many variations. This should be encouraged and followed by displaying and discussing the results.

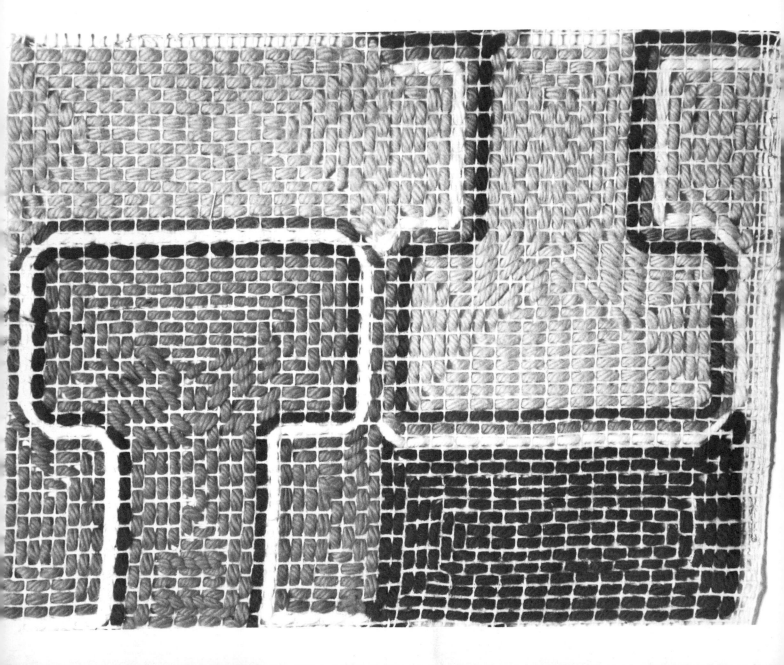

I. THE WORLD OF THE ARTIST—
The visual elements and qualities

Visual organization is important to the artist. Whether he is a painter, sculptor, printmaker, designer or craftsman, his basic tools are the *visual elements* (line, form, color, texture, space) and the *qualities* of design (unity, balance, rhythm, movement, variety). Each of these is explained in the chapter "Discovering Design."

In any work of art, all of the visual elements and qualities of design are merged or integrated into a unified organization. Although an artist may emphasize one visual element (line in a print) and it becomes a dominant characteristic of his art work,

City Scene, tempera painting.

the other visual elements are there, even if to a lesser degree.

Select examples of art work that will focus attention on the visual elements and qualities of design to broaden the children's concepts and understandings of these factors. A mobile by Alexander Calder will emphasize three-dimensional *line* (the arms), *shapes* attached to the arms and *color* used on the shapes. An etching by Rembrandt (Christ Crucified Between Two Thieves) has strong *line* qualities. *Woman with a Tie* by Modigliani shows a limited range of color, subdued tones contrasted by the strong red of the mouth.

Other examples of art may include: *Dancer on the Stage* by Edgar Degas, *The Three Puppies* by Paul Gauguin, *The Sun* by Joan Miro, *The Crab* (Steel sculpture) by Alexander Calder, *The Paris Bit* by Stuart Davis, *Night Cafe'* by Edward Hopper, *Landscape* by André Derain.

Discuss the ways in which the artist has used the visual elements and qualities to visualize his statement. How has he achieved unity or "oneness" in his art work through line? Color? Shape? What kinds of line appear in the painting or sculpture (bold, delicate, curved, straight)? What effect does color have on the observer? Is the work of art warm? Cool?

Bright? Dark? How was this achieved? In what ways do the colors relate to the idea or subject?

Discuss the artist, his work, and possibly the time in which he lived. This should be a continuing effort to develop the children's knowledge of art, artists, and the type of society in which the piece of art was created.

II. OUR ENVIRONMENT—
The role of the artist/designer in everyday life

Previous environmental emphases have been on the home, the school and the general appearance of the local community. Discussions have centered on man-made and natural components of the environment with the purpose of developing the child's perception, his awareness and his understanding of those things that combine to form the world in which he lives. The child's attention has been directed to the various spaces through which he travels and in which he lives and plays.

As a result of this closer LOOK at the immediate environment, the child should be developing some personal concepts of good and bad design in his world — an ability to discriminate between that which is attractive in contrast with the ugliness that exists in most communities.

With this background, a greater emphasis may now be placed upon some of the "treasures" of the community — those things that breathe spirit, character and interest into man's world.

Take the children on a field trip to a local park, playground, recreation center. What is it that sets these areas off as exciting and exhilarating places to go? Trees? Well-designed walk-ways? Fountains? Planting? Is it the natural beauty of the environment? Streams? A lake? What has man contributed to the esthetic appearance of these locations? Well-designed shelters? Buildings? Playground equipment?

Visit the monuments of the community. These are commemorative works of art that record events and outstanding people in history. How do they compare to environmental sculpture, displayed in outdoor spaces as decorative works of art? Sculptured pieces on a large scale and created by outstanding artists are becoming familiar parts of many of today's communities (shopping malls, parks, in green areas adjacent to new office buildings).

Schedule a field trip to buildings in the community

Crab, Alexander Calder, Museum of Fine Arts, Houston, Texas.

Chillida sculpture, Museum of Fine Arts, Houston, Texas.

that have been preserved because of their historical interest. How do these buildings compare with today's architecture? Do they help one sense the life-style of past centuries or societies?

When discussing these various trips into the community, the children may consider ways to bring their experiences to the attention of others or they may wish to promote "a better community means a better way of life". Have them draw or paint scenes of what they have observed and have an exhibit. Other creative art activities may include a mural, designing a piece of playground equipment, presenting a puppet show based on beauty in the community.

Domed Stadium, Houston, Texas.

The Cougar, by local sculptor Robert Fowler, University of Houston Student Center. Photograph courtesy Texas Highway Department.

Tempera painting, collection Children's and Young People's Classes, The Art Center, The Museum of Modern Art, New York. Photograph by James Matthews.

III. CREATIVE ART ACTIVITIES

With the children reflecting a growing maturity in various forms of visual expression, a particular emphasis at this age level may be on the visual elements (line, form, color, texture, space) and on the qualities (unity, balance, rhythm, movement, variety) that are essential to design organization. Many of these terms should by this time have become a part of the children's vocabulary and art understandings. Previous art experiences should have brought the children into contact with the works of the artist; should have assisted them toward a closer look at the natural and man-made components of the local environment; and should have provided them with opportunity to

Figure, cut and paste and tempera, age 8.

work with many different kinds of two and three dimensional materials in creating their own art. Thus, the children have had some valid bases on which to formulate their own personal concepts of design.

While the visual elements and qualities of design should not be pursued as separate entities, the art experiences programmed for this age level aim to strengthen and to build the children's concepts of these characteristics of design. For example, in painting activities a special emphasis may be on color relationships and mood; in drawing, on line and pattern; in clay work, on form and texture; in construction, on space.

Continue to encourage a spontaneous, inventive use of materials; the importance of personal expression; the significance of visual organization. Involve the children in a further understanding and knowledge of the works of the artist and an awareness of the world around them. Express enthusiasm and appreciation for the children's response to the art experience.

A. Drawing and painting

Tools and materials:

Tempera paints, large brushes, variety of 18" x 24" paper, string, sponges, small sticks, newspapers, cloths, jars for clear water.

Colored chalks, variety of papers (large sheets) including newsprint and manila drawing paper.

Wax crayons, felt pens, brushes, twigs, paper of many varieties.

Colored construction paper, cloth, yarn, cardboard, white glue, scissors, felt markers.

Emphases:

Stressing the personal nature of art expression.

Discovering new ways (techniques, processes) to give visual form to an idea or experience.

Understanding organization in design (unity of composition, emphasis, balance, action).

Building concepts of line, shape, color and texture in relation to personal interpretation. For example, how can line project a specific feeling (thin, delicate; bold, heavy) for a particular idea?

Developing skill in the use of a variety of drawing and painting media.

Painting to music, tempera, age 8.

The Chorus, tempera painting, age 9.

Tempera paint

Review the characteristics of tempera paint. Are they *opaque* or *transparent?* What does *opaque* mean? What effect does this quality have on the painting?

Discuss the mixing of colors; using primary colors (red, yellow, blue) to make secondary colors (orange, green, purple). How can a color be made lighter (tints)? Darker (shades)? Have some of the children demonstrate the mixing of colors while the rest of the class observes and comments.

Although several new painting techniques and methods for combining materials are introduced here, the most important reason for this activity remains the same as in previous age levels — *individual creative expression.* New materials and new ways to use them will stimulate the child's interest and level of response. Relating this to the child's own experiences

and imagination will help him to see art as a form of visual communications.

Talk about themes, topics and ideas that may form a basis for painting. What would the children like to paint? Organize the materials so that they are ready for use. Encourage direct painting without any preliminary sketching. This will tend to build confidence and self-reliance. If feasible, play soft background music while the children are painting. It has a relaxing, rhythmical effect on their work.

How can brightly patterned or colored cloth be combined with tempera painting to add interest? Have the children bring scraps of cloth from home. Discuss the possibilities: cutting cloth to form a dress or shirt for a figure in the painting; using cloth for an animal or a tree. Could yarn be pasted to the painting to add a strong linear or textured quality?

Pretty Feathers, tempera painting, age 8.

Provide the children with unusual painting tools, such as small, stiff twigs, tongue depressors, pieces of cellulose sponge. Demonstrate the use of such unorthodox painting tools. Discuss the results. Encourage the children to experiment.

Fun, learning and satisfaction! What would happen if the children would (1) fold a piece of drawing paper in half, (2) dip a piece of string in tempera paint, (3) open the folded paper and arrange the string over one side of the fold, leaving one end of the string extended beyond the paper, (4) fold the other side of the paper over the string (sandwiching it), (5) press one hand firmly on the paper and pull the string out?

Wax crayons can also be combined with tempera paint to produce dramatic effects. Have the children explore the possibilities: crayon design or drawing with brilliant colors, painted over with a thin mixture of dark-colored tempera. How does the tempera change the appearance of the original crayon drawing? Why does the crayon show through the tempera paint?

Trees painted with sticks and paint.

Tempera painting, age 8.

Colored chalk

Colored chalks are an especially successful medium for murals and large illustrations. They are brilliant in color and blend well by rubbing the fingers or a piece of soft cloth over the chalks.

There are a number of variations in the use of colored chalks that have quite an effect on the results. What would happen if the chalks were dipped in water and used? If the paper were made wet and dry chalks were used on the wet surface? Strange as it may seem, many artists have combined colored chalks with buttermilk. This produces a strong, permanent surface that does not flake or smear. The technique is developed by dampening the drawing paper with water, spreading a couple tablespoons of buttermilk on the surface, drawing on this with the chalk. One color can be built up over another to produce vibrant tones. When the drawing has been completed, rinse the chalks in water and place them on newspaper to dry.

Portrait, colored chalks.

Drawing, colored chalks.

Drawing

Take the children (with crayons, felt pens, white paper, and heavy pieces of cardboard to support the paper) outside of the classroom to LOOK and draw from observation. On rainy days they may go to the school cafeteria or enclosed play areas. Look for action, movement, interest — children playing, people walking, cars moving, men working, trees swaying. How can this subject matter be captured with lines on paper? Is color important? What should be included in the drawing? Omitted?

Back in the classroom have the children expand on their drawings: combining crayon and watercolor, drawing with the brush; drawing with twigs and sticks, dipped in ink or paint; combining felt pens with colored tissue. Discuss the various contrasting effects that may be produced with these combinations and tools. How may the results be applied to personal expression to achieve interest and different textural and linear effects?

Figures, crayon, age 8.

Cutting and tearing

Collage is a 20th century technique in which a number of prominent artists were involved, including Braque and Picasso. It was essentially the process of cutting or tearing paper shapes and pasting them into a desired design. Kurt Schwitters, during the early part of this century, constructed collages out of odds and ends (torn theater tickets, wrapping paper, feathers and other discards) that he found on the streets. His work, at one time, was considered anti-art. As a background for this art experience, display several examples of collage on the bulletin board.

Discuss the materials to be used (colored construction paper, magazine ads, cloth, yarn, cardboard) and how they may be transformed into design. Emphasize color, shape and texture; the overlapping of shapes to produce new shapes. How can paper be textured (wrinkling, crumpling, twisting, folding)? Talk about ideas. Suggest making a design by cutting contrasting shapes, arranging them and pasting in position on paper.

Explore the possibilities of cutting or tearing different colors of tissue paper into small shapes, crumpling them into loose wads and gluing them to the surface of a piece of drawing paper to create a design. Does this give a textural effect?

Cut paper techniques are excellent for group projects such as the making of a map showing the neighborhood — school, streets, homes, churches, streams. Shapes of paper or cloth may be cut to represent the many different components in the map.

Could cut paper and torn paper techniques be utilized in a mural project? What other materials may be combined with these techniques?

Imaginary animal, cut paper, age 8.

Collage, colored tissue paper, age 8.

125

B. Making a print

Tools and materials:
Simple tools for carving and cutting (nail file, nut pick, nails, paring knife), potatoes, oil base clay, styrofoam, plaster, brayers, water-base inks or paint pad, brushes, assorted colors of paper, newspapers, scissors.

Emphases:
Understanding the technique for making a block for printmaking by cutting the design into a surface.

Developing concepts of line, texture and color through printmaking.

Developing concepts of repetition in design.

Developing skills in printmaking.

Activities:
Prior to this, printmaking experiences have involved the children in working with scraps, gadgets and built-up plates (cardboard). The activities suggested

here require the making of a plate by incising a design into a relatively flat surface.

Perhaps because of its utter simplicity, the vegetable (potato, carrot) has become a very popular material for designing a stamp, inking it and creating a repeat pattern. While it is true that this material will demonstrate for the child the process of cutting into a surface to create a design for a print, the size of the vegetable presents certain limitations. However, for early experiences, have the children explore the potential of making repeat patterns with a design incised into the flat surface of half a potato. Paring knives, nails, nail files and nut picks are the only kinds of tools necessary for this experimental project.

Discuss the results of the design. What part of the plate actually made the print (the flat surface that remained)? Study the lines cut into the plate. How do

Repeat design print, styrofoam.

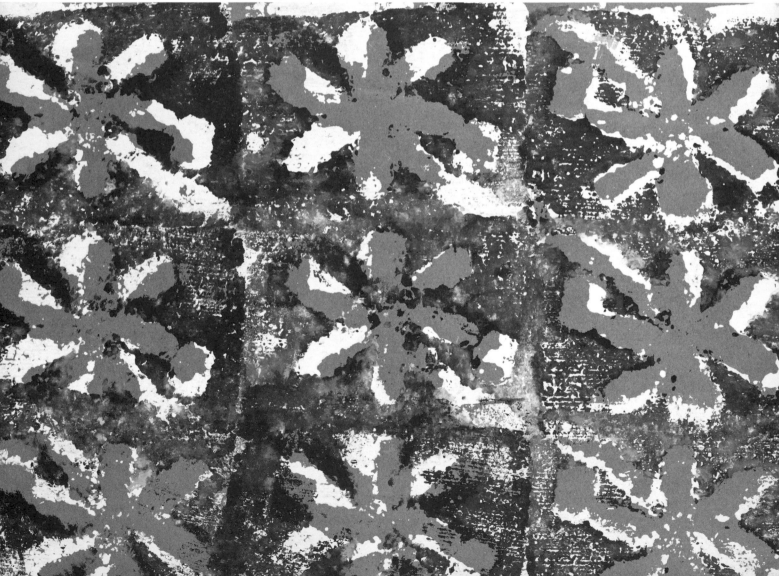

they appear in the printed design? Are they reversed? Have the children experiment with various color combinations of paint and paper, overlapping the design. Suggest combining the plates made by several children into one printed design.

Introduce other materials for making a block for printmaking. (1) *Oil base clay:* Flatten a lump of oil base clay on the tabletop. Turn the flat side up and gently press or carve a design in the clay. Brush tempera paint (mix one tablespoon of liquid starch to one cup of paint) over the surface of the clay plate. Press this against a sheet of paper to make the print. (2) *Plaster block:* Pour plaster into a cardboard lid or a milk carton (approximately 1″ thick). When the plaster hardens, remove the carton, carve the design into the surface (knives, nails), coat with shellac and when the shellac is dry, ink or paint the surface and pull a print. (3) *Styrofoam:* Synthetic materials, such as styrofoam are well within the capability of this age level for printmaking purposes. Designs may be pressed into styrofoam with nails, a nutpick or pencil.

The printmaking techniques described here are simple and effective. They are interesting and offer considerable potential for the child to discover the process of printmaking as a means for personal expression. At all times the emphasis should be on the child's design, his use of line and texture and his developing concepts of color.

Diorama of the Old West, various materials including clay.

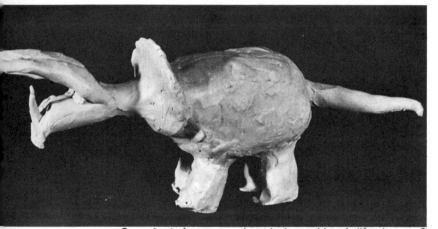
One animal of a group made to depict pre-historic life, clay, age 8.

C. Clay and group projects

Tools and materials:

Wet clay, texturing tools (nails, sticks, knives, combs), tongue depressors, modeling boards (12" x 12" pieces of vinyl or masonite), oilcloth to cover tables, sponges, water cans.

Emphases:

Modeling clay forms to depict an event; work as a group.

Developing concepts of form, proportion, texture.

Developing skill in the use of clay as a medium for personal expression.

Activities:

Previous experiences with wet clay have familiarized the children with its general characteristics and some of the basic techniques (pinch and pull, pinch-pot) utilized in creating clay forms.

Provide the children with balls of clay (size of an orange) and conduct a review by having them handle clay, shape it, cut, pull, pinch, roll it out and texture it. Be sure that the room is organized for this experience: tables covered with newspapers or oilcloth, modeling boards for each child, water and sponges for efficient clean-up.

Talk about wet clay. How can it be shaped to make a figure? An animal? What are some ways to create interesting textures on the surface of clay objects?

What would the children like to do with the clay? Suggest a group project. Discuss possible themes related to school life, the community or some aspect of the social studies program. Organize groups to plan various components of the project. Then proceed with the modeling activity. At different stages of the project, the parts should be brought together for observation and discussion.

Again, the emphasis should be on personal interpretation of ideas, creating a mood associated with the theme, and careful structuring of the clay forms. Avoid delicate details and attachments that will crack and break off. Individual pieces should be covered with wet rags or plastic bags while work is in progress. After they are completed, they may be dried at room temperature, fired and glazed.

Provision should be made for those children who would be interested in working on an individual basis or who would like to make a functional object.

Suggest pressing a ball of clay to form a pancake shape, approximately one-half inch thick and six inches in diameter. How can this be changed to form a shallow dish or bowl? What would happen to it if it were draped over a ball, a rock or a small plastic bowl? How can it be finished to be attractive? Suggest texturing the surface with the head of a large nail, a dowel, a comb, carving into the surface with a pointed stick or a knife.

D. Sand, plaster and sculptured form
Tools and materials:
Sand, molding plaster, cardboard boxes, pebbles, shells, colored glass tiles; plastic bowls.

Emphases:
Developing concepts of shape, form, texture.
Understanding a simple technique for casting.
Relating personal ideas to relief sculpture as an interesting means for visual expression.

Activity:
Although the children have had an introductory experience in sand casting earlier, the activity is one that stimulates continuing excitement and enthusiasm. In addition, the making of relief sculptures by this process requires follow-up experiences to broaden the children's understandings and skills.

Review the steps that are basic to casting a plaster form in a sand mold. (See "Casting Sand Sculpture", Age 7, Grade 2.) Organize several of the children to demonstrate. Prepare a box with a few inches of damp sand in the bottom. Talk about the possibilities of modeling figures, animals, an imaginary fish in the sand. Emphasize the importance of pressing deeply into the sand since shallow modeling will appear flat and not show as much detail. Have the demonstrators work with a spoon, sticks, and their hands to shape their design in the sand; then, mix the plaster and pour slowly over the sculptured design. The plaster should set for approximately one hour before removing from the box. Discuss the completed plaster form. How could it be improved or changed? Suggest additional work on the plaster surface with nails, knives, pointed sticks.

Talk about ideas for designing in sand. What would the children like to create? Would this be a good technique for making a mask? What kinds of people or animals would be of interest (cowboys, astronauts, dancers, athletes)? The children may make preliminary sketches or work directly in the sand. What other materials may be used to enhance the design (pebbles, shells, glass tiles)?

If the sand is available, large castings may be made directly on the ground (beaches). The children should plan the design, prepare the sand by dampening it, and proceed with the sculpturing process. Large strips of cardboard or wood may be used to frame the design and to hold the plaster in place when it is poured. A large sandcasting may be displayed as a beautiful point of interest in the school.

Relief sculpture, cast plaster combined with carving.

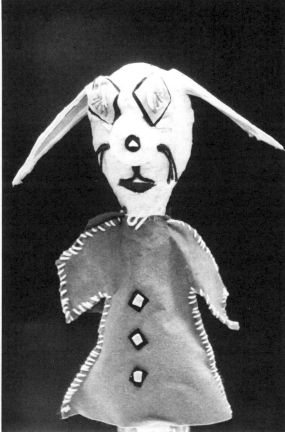

E. A sock plus imagination equals a puppet

Tools and materials:

Socks, stockings, cotton or other stuffing material, string, yarn, scraps of cloth, buttons, colored paper, scissors, glue, pins, needles and thread.

Emphases:

Developing design concepts as they relate to puppet-making.

Creating feeling, mood, character and personality in the art form, puppets.

Developing skills in the creating of puppets.

Activity:

Talk with the children about puppets as characters representing real or imaginative people or animals, as creatures of fantasy. Display and manipulate sock puppets as part of the motivation. Invite some of the children to use the puppets. Ideas will start flowing. A puppet in the hands of a child soon becomes a "live" creature through which the child naturally projects his thoughts and feelings.

Use stories, poems, music, experiences of the children as bases for puppet-making activities. The whole meaning of this experience reaches a higher level of significance when it becomes more than simply making a puppet; when it results in a dramatic event with colorful characters, scenery, script and finally a gala presentation in the school. In this way the puppet experience strengthens speech skills, personality and creative thought of the children.

The basic unit for this puppet-making activity is the sock or stocking. Children may bring these from home. Have the children slip their hands into socks with their fingers all the way to the toe and with the heel resting on the back of the hand. Ask the children to move their fingers, wrist and arm to see what kind of action they can produce. What does this suggest? An alligator? A snake? A dragon? How can the socks be changed to achieve greater representation of the animals or figures? Where will stuffing be needed? How can the eyes, nose, and mouth be made?

Discuss the possibilities for converting socks into "people puppets". Demonstrate tying the sock first below the heel. The foot part can be cut into thin strips to represent hair. Stuff the section below the tied part to make the puppet head. Leave enough opening in the neck for the child's finger. Have the child push the stuffing around until he can move the head by wiggling his finger. The thumb and third finger will then become the puppet's arms. A small slit cut into either side of the sock will allow the thumb and finger to come through. How can a dress or coat be made and added? Discuss the decoration of the head: large ears, yarn for hair, a hat or turban, the nose and eyes.

Consider dividing the class into groups to make specific characters for a puppet play related to school activities, geography, reading, mathematics. When preparations have been completed for the big dramatic presentation, invite parents to attend. Through this project they will become more aware of the innate ability of the children, the research and learning that is taking place.

F. Masks, ceremony and customs

Tools and materials:
Newspapers, wax paper, aluminum foil, masking tape, decorative materials (yarn, beads, buttons, raffia, scraps), wheat paste, cardboard.

Emphases:
Understanding the significance of masks to primitive cultures, to present day celebrations.

Developing concepts of shape, form and color as they relate to this art form.

Developing skills in the use of art materials.

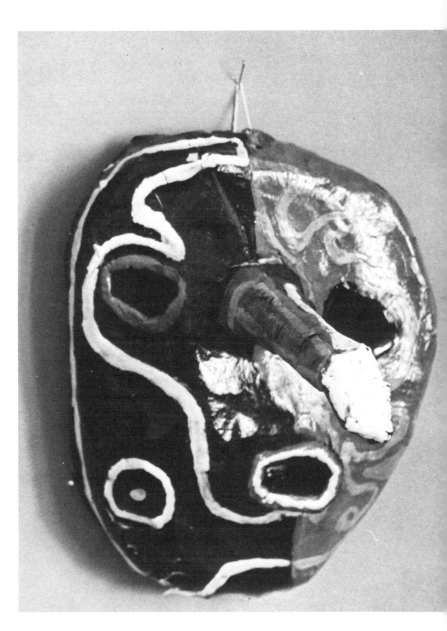

Activity:

Display examples of masks used by primitive cultures. Why did they make masks? How did the masks reflect the customs of a particular culture? Talk about the designs of different masks and how they have influenced present-day artists and designers. Refer to the Indians of North and South America and how they have retained the use of masks for many of their ancient and still observed ceremonial customs. This is also true of primitive people of Africa, Australia and islands of the South Pacific (Easter Island). Actual masks may be seen in most museums. Prints and films of masks may be used to motivate children, to help them gain insights and ideas for their own personal involvement in mask-making.

How can the mask be used today in the local community? Although ceremonial masks are not generally a part of the 20th century American culture, there are numerous occasions where the mask does play a significant role. Perhaps one of the most widely publicized events is the Mardi Gras in New Orleans. Talk about the mask in relation to holidays, carnivals, school plays. Another interesting theme would be designing masks to reflect life today — contemporary masks, commenting on business, industry, society. What kinds of materials may be used (electronic parts, wire, newspaper ads)? Challenge the imagination of the children by having them design masks based on creatures of outer space.

One technique for making a mask would be to use a piece of cardboard (larger than the intended size of the mask) as a base for the form. Draw a large oval on the cardboard. Using crumpled newspaper and masking tape, build up the surface to create a form somewhat like a football cut in half lengthwise. Cover this with a sheet of aluminum foil, pressing the foil around the form and down against the cardboard. This should be covered with wax paper so that the mask that will be constructed over the form may be easily removed. Tear newspaper pages into strips approximately one inch wide (tear down the long dimension of the page). Dip the strips in creamy thick wheat paste and place them one by one over the prepared form. Overlap and crisscross the strips of paper, smoothing them carefully and extending them down on to the cardboard base. Build up several layers of newspaper strips to give strength to the mask. As this paper shell dries, it will retain its form. Small boxes or crumpled balls of newspaper may be added to shape features of the mask such as the nose. These should be attached by running paper strips, dipped in wheat paste, over them.

After this stage of the mask has been completed, allow it to dry and remove it by slipping a knife between the cardboard base and the mask. If the mask is to be worn, cut holes into it for the eyes.

The real excitement comes during the time of decorating the surface of the mask. Have many different materials (tempera paints, yarn, beads, buttons, found objects, raffia, steel wool) available for the children to explore. Discuss. What materials best project the character of the mask? How may they be attached? Talk about the mood created with bright colors in contrast with dull colors; the possibilities of steel wool, yarn, raffia for hair. The completed masks should be sprayed with shellac or clear plastic spray.

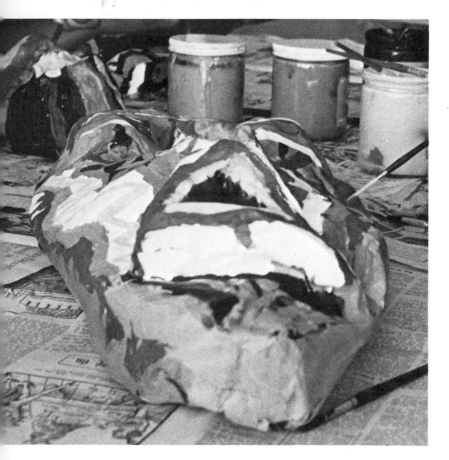

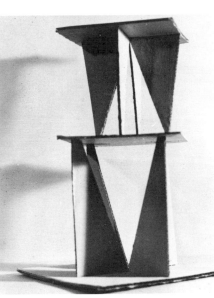

Cardboard construction
emphasizing the repeated shape.

G. Constructed sculpture

Tools and materials:

Wood of various sizes and shapes, scraps of wood, string, yarn, fast-drying glue, styrofoam, cardboard, plaster of Paris, tempera paints, brushes, hammers, saws, small nails (brads), tacks.

Emphases:

Discovering new, three-dimensional forms.

Developing concepts of space and three-dimensional form; color and line qualities.

Activities:

Unusual materials often serve as a motivational agent in the developing of children's concepts of design and in expanding their perception and awareness. Many of the materials suggested for creating sculptural forms by constructing, are discards — by-products or parts of products (for example, spools that once held thread; odd pieces of lumber usually tossed into a scrap box) that daily find their way to the city dump. Twentieth century artists have often used such items as wheels, gears, common hardware and assorted abandoned items in creating sculpture and assemblages. Picasso is noted for his three-dimensional creations, unique and frequently amusing.

Provide a special place in the room for a large box to store a variety of odds and ends that may be used in constructing projects. Encourage the children to bring in wood scraps from the lumberyard or father's workshop, spools, dowels, applicator sticks, and

other things that they feel might apply.

Show examples of assemblages (Louise Nevelson) and constructions (Naum Gabo, Antoine Pevsner, Constantin Brancusi). These outstanding artists are usually well represented in most art books that describe 20th century art.

Select a number of items from the scrap box and display them on a table as a basis for discussion. Talk about different shapes, sizes and textures. Have the children handle and combine several pieces that are of special interest to them. What does this suggest? Soon other children will "see" things in the materials and will start to associate their own ideas with various combinations. Discuss different ways for fastening pieces together (glue, nails, string). How can color be used to create interest? Or should the natural qualities of the materials be retained? As the children develop their constructions, stress unity (oneness of design), balance, and proportion (relationship of parts to each other). Some of the constructions may develop from a wood base; others may be built to stand on their own projections or be suspended on a string to turn slowly in space.

Several children may be interested in building a sculptural form with styrofoam and plaster. Strips and pieces of styrofoam may be joined by gluing or with pins or toothpicks. Use a heavy cardboard base. Suggest pushing sticks into the styrofoam to add height. How can string be incorporated into the design to produce linear qualities? Could shapes of cardboard be used to add solid areas? After this phase of the sculpture has been completed as the child desires, have him prepare the plaster to a creamy consistency. Suggest dripping the plaster over the construction. What happens? The plaster may also be modeled with a stick over the flat surfaces. Should color (tempera paint) be used?

Space Station, collection the Children's and Young People's Classes, The Art Center, The Museum of Modern Art, New York.

H. Lettering

Tools and materials:

Newspapers, colored construction paper, tempera paints, flat bristle brushes, wide-nib felt pens, yarn, paste, scissors, straight pins.

Emphases:

Developing skill in lettering, using various materials and techniques.

Understanding the structure of letters.

Understanding the importance of spacing to legibility.

Activities:

Lettering experiences here should be a follow-up to those the children had at a previous age level. Display examples of lettering on the bulletin board. Discuss the structure of letters, spacing to form legible words, spacing between words. What are some of the uses of lettering? How can lettering be used in the school: bulletin board titles and captions, signs, names on booklets and portfolios?

Lettering is one of the most useful and versatile forms of graphic expression. Good lettering enhances the appearance of notebooks, charts, posters, bulletin boards and school announcements. There will be many opportunities for the children to use their lettering skills. Provision should be made for them to practice. Avoid alphabet charts. Emphasize direct application.

Three different sets of materials or lettering tools are suggested here.

Flat bristle brushes and tempera paint: Use the same materials and directions recommended for the seven-year child earlier in this book. Larger brushes at least 1" wide will offer a new challenge.

Wide-nib felt pens: Felt pens with wide, chisel-shaped nibs can be obtained in a variety of colors. In many respects, these are much easier for children to use for lettering than the flat bristle brush. Equal in importance to understanding the structure of letters is the achieving of skill in handling the tools. Have the children experiment by making different practice strokes (vertical, horizontal, diagonal, curved). This may be done on the classified ad section of the newspaper, using the column lines as guidelines. Have the children letter their names and simple signs: Keep the School Clean, Walk, Don't Run. Stress the importance of parallel guidelines to maintain a straight line of letters and to assure that all letters in a single word are the same height.

Cut paper letters: Provide the children with strips of paper 1/2" wide and 3" to 4" long. Discuss with them the possibilities of forming letters with these strips. Straight letters such as the I, L, and T will be rather simple to make. How does the W, X, and A differ from these? Can they be made with the 1/2" strips of paper? Will it be possible to make the O, C, B, and S with these same pieces of paper? How will they have to be cut? Combine demonstration with the children's searching efforts. Paper should be available so the children can paste down the letters while making them. Try using various color combinations: yellow letters on black paper, orange on red. Note the effect of these color combinations on the legibility of the letters.

Additional materials that are interesting for lettering include: (1) Yarn cut and pasted to paper to form letters. (2) Colored pipe cleaners may be bent in the shape of letters and glued to a cardboard background. Encourage experimentation.

An interesting spin-off of lettering activities is the designing of collages with a variety of letters cut from magazine and newspaper ads. The purpose of this experience would not be to form words but to arrange and paste letters in various positions to create a design.

Letters from left, heavy cord, broken applicator sticks, pipe cleaner, brush and paint on newspaper.

I. Textiles—woven and stitched
Tools and materials:

Weaving: Wood frames, string or warp thread, yarn, natural grasses, raffia, small finishing nails, hammer, ruler.

Stitchery: Burlap, pieces of printed cloth, embroidery thread, yarns; darning needles, pins, scissors.

Emphases:

Weaving: Learning the technique of weaving; developing concepts of design (texture, color, shape) in relation to the woven form.

Stitchery: Understanding various stitches utilized in designing on cloth; understanding the difference between designing on cloth (stitchery) and making the design an integral part of the cloth (weaving); developing concepts of shape and color.

Activities:

Weaving: Discuss the fundamentals of weaving. Show examples. What is the warp thread? What is meant by the term, "weft"? Talk about design.

Frame looms are commercially made and may be purchased ready for use. On the other hand it is quite possible for the children to make their own looms. A smooth picture frame, a wooden box approximately three inches deep or four smooth sticks nailed to form a rectangle will serve the purpose. Space finishing nails, 1/4" apart, across the two short ends of the frame. The nails should be slanted a bit to prevent the warp thread from slipping off. One inch of free space should remain along each side.

Have the children warp the looms with strong string or warping thread. They should start by tying a knot around one of the corner nails. Then pull the string to the opposite end and go around the outside of the first two nails. Pull the string back to the starting end and go around the second and third nails, then back to the other end and around the third and fourth nails. This procedure should be continued until the entire loom is warped.

Now start the weaving process. Yarn may be tied to a flat bobby pin or a tapestry needle to facilitate the movement back and forth, over and under the warp threads. Caution the children to keep the yarn loose as each row is completed. If the yarn is pulled too tight, the weaving will be pulled out of shape. Have the children experiment with different colors of yarn. As the color is changed, tie the new color to the one just woven. Be careful to tie the knot on the underside of the weaving.

How can other materials be woven into the design to add interest? Experiment.

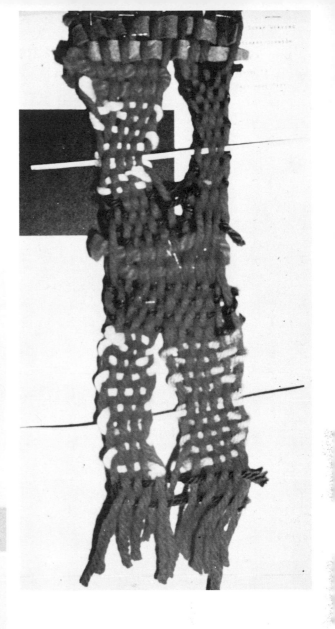

Weaving on board loom (board and nails).
Photograph by David Donoho.

Stitchery: Display examples of stitchery. Discuss the design. Are all of the stitches used in the design the same? How do different kinds of stitches create interest? Provide the children with small pieces of burlap, lightweight yarn and darning needles. Have them practice making stitches — "drawing" on the burlap with yarn. Discuss the results of their efforts. Demonstrate the making of a few basic stitches. The running stitch is the simplest. Have some of the children demonstrate stitches that they have mastered.

Discuss possible themes or ideas that may be developed with stitches on burlap. Designs may first be planned with crayon on paper and then transferred to the burlap to be stitched. Emphasize the importance of using the entire piece of burlap; contrasting colors of yarn. Encourage the children to experiment. Could shapes (figures, animals, houses, trees or just interesting shapes) be cut from felt or pieces of patterned cloth and sewn onto the burlap to form part of the design (appliqué)?

Stitchery pieces may be made for such purposes as place mats, center pieces, and wall hangings.

Painting, crayon-tempera resist, age 6.

Weaving, age 11.

Painting, tempera, age 8.

Lion, papier-mâché, age 10.

Circus, ink and cut paper, age 10.

Puppets and stage, age 9.

Masks, papier-mâché, age 11.

Stage design and costume, age 10.

Mural,
ceramic tiles,
age 10.

Painting, tempera, age 8.

THE MATURING CHILD
AGES 9-11 (GRADES 4-6)

The quality of the child's earlier art experiences serves as a springboard for his ability to respond and to achieve in the latter part of his elementary school art education. His concepts of design, his skill in the selection and use of tools and materials for personal graphic expression, his understanding and appreciation of the art of others, his reaction to his environment, and his ability to make design judgments are put to the test. The art program in the upper elementary school is an extension and expansion of the child's previous art learnings and should lead him into a deeper understanding of the world of art and a higher regard for his own graphic expression.

Characteristics of the maturing child

The rate of growth and development of the older child is characterized by variations that are not too different from that of the younger child. Such

dissimilarities, reflected in the graphic image produced by the child and in his response to the art experience, reinforce the need to consider each child as an individual. For at any single grade or age level this differentiation of capabilities within a group of children may extend above or below what may be thought of as the "norm".

Yet there are some distinguishable characteristics that reflect the visual and expressive development of the child within this age range, assuming that his previous art experiences have been favorable:

• *Greater comprehension of art problems and individualistic and imaginative response.*

• *Desire for representation (realism), concern for detail and "rightness" in his art work.*

• *Increasing skill in handling of art tools and materials.*

• *Interest in art techniques and art processes.*

• *Greater sensitivity to color, line, shape, form, texture and the visual qualities of design (unity, balance, rhythm, movement, variety); a developing sense of order and composition; greater visual awareness.*

• *Desire to experiment with materials; to search and discover new ways to use art materials.*

• *Relating art to other interests — science, outer space, world events.*

Crayon and wash drawing, age 11.

"The New York Subway", painting, age 11.

The maturing child is more cooperative with others; respects their efforts; shares materials, ideas. He is an increasingly responsible individual, has a longer period of concentration, is energetic, enthusiastic, pleased with his successes — but often self-critical.

Expected behavioral changes

• *The child understands and utilizes more complex skills, techniques, and processes in his visual expression.*

• *The child comprehends a variety of styles of visual interpretation.*

Linoleum block print, age 11.

- *The child makes critical analysis of his art work and the art work of others.*

- *The child responds to his environment, identifies visual defects, and searches for appropriate solutions.*

- *The child is increasingly knowledgeable of the art of history and of today, the diversity of style and forms of art expression.*

- *The child grows in his understanding of design concepts.*

- *The child increases his art vocabulary.*

Program of art experiences

Continuing on the premise that art experiences in the elementary schools should provide the child with opportunities for self-expression, should lead him to the thrill of discovery, and should assure him a sense of fulfillment, the following program represents a sequence of activities, materials, understandings, and concepts that are an extension of art experiences of the primary grades. Emphasizing greater depth and a higher degree of complexity in skills, techniques and content, every effort has been made to introduce new and challenging (to the child) art experiences (ideas, materials, techniques, processes) at each age level.

This program of art experiences does not attempt to exhaust all of the possibilities for the elementary school art program. Nor is it a rigid scheme designed to solve all of the problems or needs encountered in the classroom. It is a suggested direction, containing a flexibility by which it may be adapted to most school needs.

The program coordinates information related to APPRECIATION, ENVIRONMENT, and ART ACTIVITIES at each grade level.

Paper sculpture mask, age 11.

153

AGE 9—(GRADE 4)
AN EVER EXPANDING WORLD

Horizontal Spines, mobile sculpture by Alexander Calder. In collection of Addison Gallery, Phillips Academy, Andover, Massachusetts.

I. THE WORLD OF THE ARTIST—*Materials, tools, techniques*

The artist has used many different kinds of materials and tools to express his ideas and experiences in a personal way.

Three or four good reproductions, prominently displayed in the classroom should be sufficient to start a good discussion growing out of the interest and curiosity of the child. Selection of examples should be based on a diversity of materials, techniques and styles. For example: (1) *Mobile* by Alexander Calder; metal shapes painted strong, bright colors and attached to wire arms. (2) *Reclining Figure* by Henry Moore; solidity and heaviness of simplified stone and bronze figures. (3) *Man and Dog in Front of Sun* by Joan Miro; colorful, gay, childlike, poetic painting in oils; flat, bright colors and shapes. (4) *Women and Dog* by Marisol; wood, plaster and miscellaneous items; whimsical, boxlike forms.

Provide time for the children to talk about these art works and have them try to identify the materials used by the artist. How did the artist use specific materials to give shape to his ideas? How did the materials influence or limit the artist? Some materials like paint and wet clay are flowing or pliable; others such as stone and wood are hard and rigid. What effect does this have on the artist as he creates? How does this relate to the materials used by the children in their own drawing, painting, and three-dimensional activities?

When possible, these classroom discussions should be supplemented by trips to the museum or to works of art located in the community where the child can see the actual art product and the materials used to create it. Further reference to the influence and nature of materials and tools of the artist should be considered when the children are using brushes, crayons, paper, paint, clay, wire, cloth, in classroom art activities.

II. OUR ENVIRONMENT . . .
Buildings in the community

Direct the attention of the child to old and new homes, public buildings, churches, places of business, industry, shopping centers; concrete, wood, stone, brick, steel, glass, new materials.

A community is comprised of many kinds of buildings serving a wide variety of purposes. What are some of the outstanding buildings in the local community?

Why have some buildings been removed and replaced with new structures while others have been re-modeled or refurbished (preservation because of historical or cultural values)? Discuss the function of specific buildings in the community. Invite a local architect in to talk to the children about architecture — tools and materials of the architect; the enclosing of space for specific purposes; the use of art in public buildings — sculpture, painting, murals.

Take the children on a walk through the community. This may be merely a SEEING experience or they may sketch, paint or photograph buildings that have special appeal to them. An interesting classroom problem would be to have the children redesign a building that they have seen or sketched. This activity should be kept at an elementary level and should be presented to challenge the child's imagination rather than seek technical accuracy.

Display pictures of buildings on the classroom bulletin board. One approach would be to select buildings from different cultures to show striking contrasts — Egyptian Temple, Gothic Cathedral, the Astro-dome in Houston, examples of new buildings in almost any city's urban renewal areas.

Photograph of the burned house.

Fourth graders sketching the remains of a burned house in the vicinity of school.

Felt pen sketch by one of the ten-year-old children.

Drawing, charcoal, age 9.

Cut paper design — pattern in repetition. Construction paper and paste, age 9.

III. CREATIVE ART ACTIVITIES

How do materials influence us in what we do in art? In what ways do materials assist in the expressing of an idea? Are we limited by the materials in how we say something visually? Some art materials, such as paints, are fluid. Chalks are dry and powdery; crayons, waxy. Still other materials including clay, wire, paper, and cloth are pliable, flexible. Provide opportunity for the children to experiment and to discover for themselves the potential and limitations of various two- and three-dimensional materials. This should include, where appropriate, the combining of materials to determine the effect of one on the other and how this technique may be utilized in personal visual expression.

A. Sketching, drawing, painting

Tools and materials:

Felt pens, ball-point pens, crayons, chalks, large soft-lead pencils.
Tempera paints.
Colored papers, newspaper (classified ad section),

newsprint, kraft paper, white drawing paper.

Small sponges, brayers, textured items (mesh, corrugated board, burlap, coarse sandpaper), brushes, scissors, paste.

Emphases:

Discovering the potential of materials.

Experimenting with simple combinations: crayon and paint; light colors on dark colored paper; felt pen and tempera.

Creating texture and pattern with line.

Using different kinds of line to create mood or interest. (Bold, thick lines in contrast with thin, delicate lines; straight lines opposed to curved; solid to broken; horizontal to sharp angular).

Strengthening color concepts including INTENSITY (brightness or dullness of color), VALUE (lightness or darkness); WARM colors (reds, oranges, yellows); cool colors (blues, purples, greens).

Activities:

Any or all of the materials listed may be made available to the children. If it is feasible, the class should be organized into groups, one group using felt pens; a second, drawing with crayons; a third, chalks; a fourth, paints. When viewing the results, the children will see immediately the influence of materials on the work that they have done.

Textured materials should be made available to children using soft-lead pencils and crayons. Encourage experimentation with such materials by placing them beneath the paper and rubbing the pencil or crayon over the surface. Discuss how the textured results may be adapted to specific art problems.

Although brushes of various sizes will continue to be used in painting, suggest the use of sponges or brayers for backgrounds or large areas of color. Have the children wrap string around the brayer and roll paint on the paper. Put a little glycerin in the paint to retard drying. Encourage some children to use felt pens or colored chalks over the tempera paint backgrounds.

Suggest using chalk on wet paper, rough textured paper; chalk dipped in water and used on dry paper; bright colors of chalk on dark paper; using the broad side of the crayon; notching the side of the crayon and dragging it across the paper; using the side of the pencil point.

An interesting technique: Have the children create a variety of shapes with different colors of crayon on

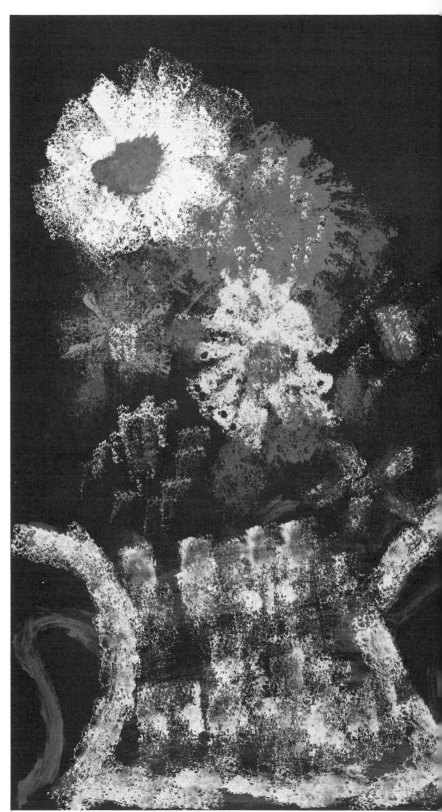

Sponge painting, age 9.

Various patterns created by placing textured materials under paper and rubbing over with crayons.

paper. The shapes should be placed close to each other. After the paper has been covered completely, place it upside down on a plain piece of paper and draw on the reverse side with a blunt stick, the end of a brush or a ball-point pen. What happens?

Have some children develop their drawings with white crayon on white paper or yellow crayon on yellow paper. Then suggest that they brush a single contrasting color of thinned tempera paint over the entire surface. Surprise! This may lead into a variation where the child will complete a wax crayon drawing, dampen the paper, ball it up rather tightly, flatten it out on a pad of newspapers, and apply a solid coat of thinned tempera paint. By washing the surface with clear water, the crinkled effect of batik will result.

Suggest cutting or tearing colored paper to make the objects or figures for a picture. The child would then arrange these shapes on a piece of background paper, pasting them in the desired positions. Felt pens or ball-point pens may be used to add details.

These are just a few experimental activities that will strengthen the children's understandings of the potential or limitations of art materials. At the same time such activities will assist in the development of individual skills. Much of the excitement, pleasure, and motivation that children receive from art experiences occurs in a learning environment that supports search and experimentation and leads to new discoveries.

The art concepts and knowledge acquired through experimental activities should be related to specific art problems:

Scenes in the local environment

Discuss natural and man-made forms in the local environment. A particular emphasis may be placed on local architecture which may range from a simple, weathered shed to a church building, interesting houses in the vicinity of the school building, a new shopping center, or a building partially destroyed by fire. Take the children outside to sketch in the vicinity of the school. Talk about the scene. If it is a building, discuss the total form of the structure; windows, doors, brick, wood, glass, cement; the general impression — is it old, new, bright, dull, warm and alive? Observe the sky, clouds, color, shadow, trees, street, poles, signs, people, traffic.

Art works (reproductions, slides) that may be used to supplement this study include *Rainy Night* by Charles Burchfield, *Midnight Ride of Paul Revere* by Grant

Wood, *Liberation* by Ben Shahn. These paintings contain architecture but treated in different ways. Another painting that relates and would have special appeal to the children is *Children's Games* by Pieter Brueghel, 16th century Flemish painter. Paintings by Edward Hopper and John Sloan, 20th century American artists would also be of interest.

Single objects (shells, toys, tools, found objects that have special interest for the child)

These should be readily available to the child so that he can handle, feel, examine and draw or paint at close proximity. Discuss general shape, surface quality, color and structure of the object.

Two contrasting paintings are *After the Hunt* by William Michael Harnett, late 19th century American and *Dahlias and Pomegranates* by Henri Matisse, 20th century French. Discuss Harnett's extremely realistic interpretation of subject matter; Matisse's concern for line and color relationships, surface pattern.

Fantasy

A dream, interpretation of music, illustration of a story or poem; wild stories; draw or paint a surprise.

Show the children examples of art that may be considered imaginative, fanciful, unreal, such as *Large Composition* by Joan Miro,' *The Persistence of Memory* by Salvadore Dali, *Threatening Weather* by Rene Margritte; three artists representing Surrealism and presenting dream-like qualities in their painting.

Painting of a city scene, paint combined with ink, age 9.

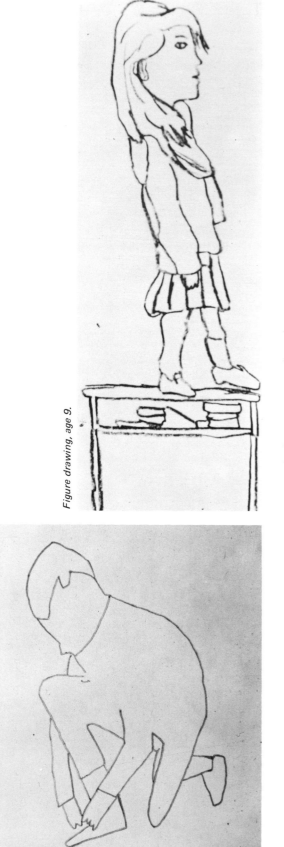

Figure drawing, age 9.

Figure drawing (contour), age 9.

Self-portraits

Children may draw or paint themselves by looking into mirrors, if available; or draw themselves as they think they are; may also draw or paint themselves as fictitious characters or to appear as what they would want to be (fireman, athlete, nurse, movie actress, rancher, cowboy). An interesting variation would be for the children to draw themselves on a secret mission or soaring away from the earth in a space ship. Encourage a simple direct approach; emphasis on outstanding features and self-identification.

Art works that relate include *Senecio* by Paul Klee, 20th century — relatively flat patterns of color, geometric shapes. *Lady at the Tea Table* by Mary Cassatt who studied with the French Impressionists. *Self Portrait* by Albrecht Dürer, 16th century, the Renaissance in the North and a new realism. *Troubled Man* by Ben Shahn, 20th century American; feeling and an economy of line. *Self-portrait with Seven Fingers* by Marc Chagall, 20th century Russian Jew influenced by Cubism and known for the dream-like fantasy qualities in his painting. Four portraits and a range of style!

The figure, seated, stooping, standing, throwing

Have the class take these different positions to experience the action of the body. One child may then be used as a model. Discuss the general proportions of the figure — relationship of arms to body, size of head in relation to height of the posed model, action of the figure. Encourage a free, spirited approach to catch the feeling of the pose. Have the model hold something: a flag, a stick, a book, a shopping bag.

Look at a variety of art works in which the figure is dominant including *Sunday Afternoon on the Island of the Grande Jatte* by Georges Seurat, 19th century French pointilist. *Lamentation* by Giotto, 14th century Italian. *The Card Players* by Paul Cézanne, late 19th century French and often referred to as the precursor of modern art. *Pleasures, Homage to Louis-David* by Fernand Leger, 20th century French influenced by Cubism. These paintings show how different artists at various times in history have interpreted the figure. Drawings by Matisse, Picasso, and Daumier are suggested for additional study related to the figure.

Yarn print, age 9. Yarn glued to cardboard surface, inked and printed.

B. Making a print

Tools and materials:

Finger paints, oilcloth and paper.

Textured fabrics, wire mesh, string, tree bark, leaves, man-made objects, heavy cardboard, paper, water base printing ink, ink slab (glass or formica), brayers, glue.

Paper, scissors, water base ink, brayers, glass or formica ink slabs.

Emphases:

Experimenting with simple printmaking processes.
Using color, shape, and textures to create a design.
Strengthening concepts of shape and repetition to achieve harmony and unity in design.
Broadening concepts of printmaking, that is, pressuring paper against a prepared surface to produce a design.

Activities:

Three different sets of materials are listed here to provide children printmaking experiences that will produce varied results. The printmaking process suggested by the materials is basically monoprinting or making a single print. However, the second group of materials (textured items) may be used to make a printing plate from which several prints may be made.

Fingerpaint print, age 9.

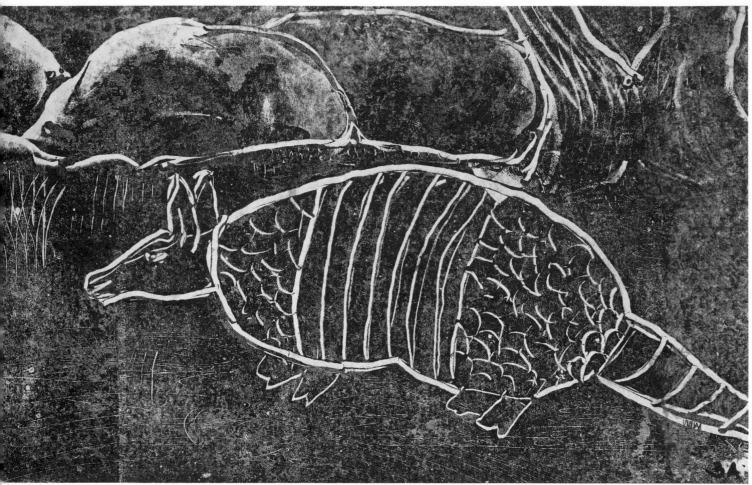

Monoprint made by scraping and wiping into ink rolled on ink slab and pressuring paper over design, age 9.

It is suggested that the class be divided into three groups, each group working with a different combination of materials. If desirable, children may move from one activity to another in order to have an opportunity to experiment with more than one set of materials.

Group One. Finger paint designs may be made directly on oilcloth covering the table. While the design is wet, place a piece of paper over it and apply pressure over the back of the paper with the palm of the hand or a clean brayer. Lift the paper and see the print.

Group Two. Designs may be made by inking single textured objects and pressuring against a sheet of paper. Children may also select various textured items and arrange them into a design on a sheet of heavy cardboard. These may be fixed in position with glue. After the glue has dried, the resultant printing plate may be inked with a brayer and a print made by

pressuring paper against the surface. Another way to make a print from this kind of plate is to place a piece of paper on it, rolling an inked brayer over the paper.

Group Three. Using a brayer, have the children roll a thin coat of water soluble printing ink on the glass or formica ink slab. The design is developed by arranging shapes of paper on the inked slab, placing a large sheet of paper over this and pressuring with the palm of the hand or a clean brayer.

Following a time of experimentation with the materials, discuss ways by which these techniques may be used to express an idea. How can interest, action, and unity of design be achieved through repeated shapes; contrast in color and size of shape? Is it possible or desirable to use any of these printmaking techniques to reproduce subject matter such as houses, people, animals? How does this form of expression relate to painting activities?

Textured print.

Print made with textured objects, age 9.

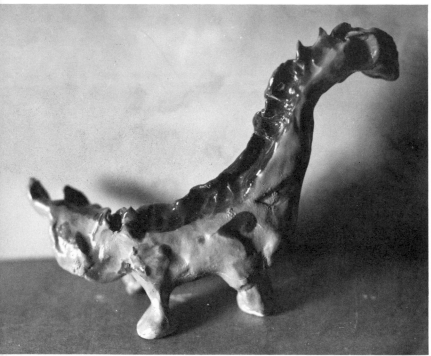

Clay animal.

Clay pot with part of surface designed by adding clay coils and small lumps of clay.

Pot made by clay coil construction.

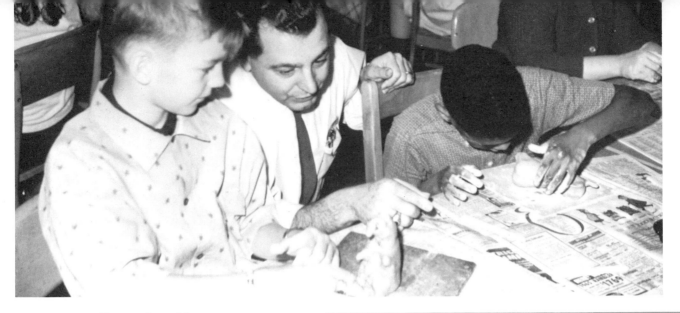

C. Clay coils and an idea

Tools and materials:

Wet clay, tables covered with oilcloth, small masonite boards 12″ x 12″ (modeling boards), water, sticks.

Emphases:

Creating clay forms, functional or non-functional, with clay coils.

Broadening earlier concepts of design in terms of three-dimensional form.

Developing skill in the use of clay as material for personal expression.

Activities:

Discuss with the children some of the characteristics of clay — its plasticity, softness, and how it may be shaped, rolled, bent, textured, smoothed. Suggest experimental activity in which the clay is rolled out, forming rope-like lengths. How may these strips or coils of clay be used to construct an object or a form? Would it be possible to make a bowl or a small pot by building the sides with coils of clay? Can the same technique be used to construct a figure or an animal? In what way can the coil technique be combined with the pinch pot method learned at a lower grade level?

Children may experiment further by winding coils of clay around a short length of cardboard tubing or a cylindrical bottle. Upon completion, remove the tubing or bottle. What can be added to transform this basic form into a creature of fantasy? A container? How may the surface of the finished object be smoothed or textured to create interest?

Show examples (actual or photographs) of sculpture, pottery.

Clay coils added to form part of surface decoration. Textured qualities in lower part made by pressing into coils with a stick.

D. Forms with paper

Tools and materials:

Wheat paste, old newspapers, small boxes of various sizes and shapes, cardboard tubing, string, tape, scissors, paints, brushes, and a variety of decorative materials (yarn, cloth, buttons, etc.)

Emphases:

Building a three-dimensional form with paper.
Developing an imaginative response through a specific three-dimensional technique.
Relating design concepts such as color, texture, and shape to an art form.

Activities:

Many sizes, colors and textures of paper are used in art expression. Perhaps the greatest use of paper is in drawing and painting activities. Yet some of the most exciting art activities involve the transforming of paper from a flat two-dimensional quality into three-dimensional forms.

Discuss the possibilities of building a three-dimensional form with strips of paper soaked in wheat paste. Two basic techniques may be considered. These may have application in the making of masks, animals, figures. In either procedure, the important part of the experience is the child's idea and how he expresses it visually in terms of the papier-mâché strip method. Themes or topics for motivation may be based on stories, songs, plays, social studies units, holidays.

One approach is to create the form (animal, figure, mask) with clay. Strips of newspaper dipped in wheat paste, mixed to a creamy consistency, are wrapped over and around the clay object. This should be built up to several layers. After the paste has dried, cut the form open and remove the clay. The hollow shell may then be rejoined by taping it together and adding strips of paper soaked in wheat paste. Generally, the papier-mâché shell will slip off a clay mask rather easily, without having to be cut.

Another technique is to start with a basic core of crumpled paper held together with string or small boxes, applying several layers of newspaper strips as above. The resultant form may grow out of the child's preconceived idea or, as an interesting form in itself, may suggest a specific object or direction for the child. If the child's goal is to make a mask, the ears, nose, eyes and mouth may be formed by building up and modeling (with paper) on the surface

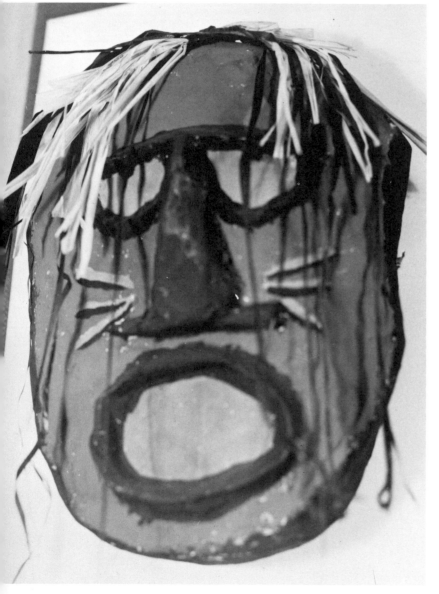

where he desires. Appendages (arms, legs, heads) for animals and figures may be made with rolls of newspaper, cardboard tubes, and elongated boxes. These may be attached to the basic form with staples, string, or tape. As these parts are added, the papier-mâché strips should be applied to strengthen and unify the total form. Action and ability to stand alone are important goals in the making of papier-mâché animals and figures.

Talk about ways to decorate the surface of the completed paper form. How can color be used to add vitality, expressiveness, interest? In what ways can other materials, such as yarn, string, felt, cloth, buttons, raffia, and discarded costume jewelry, be used?

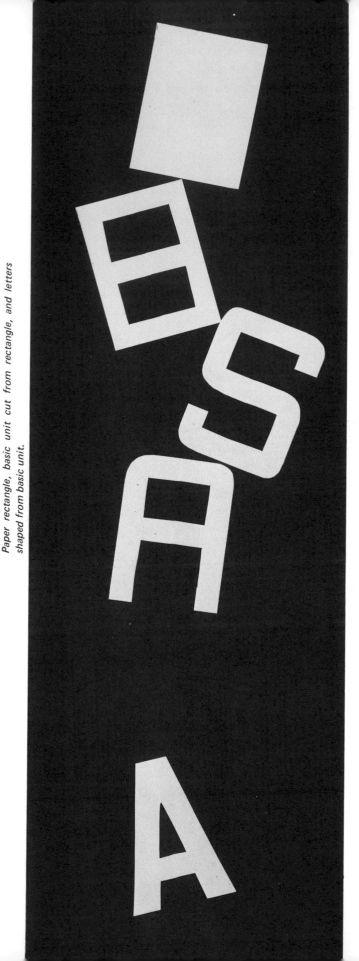

Paper rectangle, basic unit cut from rectangle, and letters shaped from basic unit.

E. A word is . . .

Tools and materials:

Various colors of construction paper, scissors, pins, bulletin board, paste, poster board.

Emphases:

Developing understanding of a simple gothic letter.
Developing basic concepts of lettering and skill in constructing to form words.
Making application of the lettered word.

Activities:

Discuss the significance of lettering in everyday life — signs, billboards, displays in store windows, packaging, posters. Display a wide variety of lettering on the bulletin board for the purposes of motivating interest and formulating understandings. What are some of the differences observed in lettering? How does lettering express mood, feeling (delicate letters, bold letters)? Is color important? Size? How is lettering used in the school?

For classroom experiences, focus attention on one simple style, preferably the Gothic capital alphabet. Other styles and lowercase letters may be considered later as desired. The Gothic letter is generally a straight, plain letter with all parts of uniform thickness.

Although letters may be made with many kinds of tools and materials (brush, pen, crayon, chalk, string, yarn), suggest the cut paper technique. This is perhaps one of the most versatile and interesting methods.

Discuss uniformity of size which is important to readability. Start with a strip of paper, the height of which will represent the height of the letters to be cut. For each letter in a word, cut one rectangle from the strip. Each rectangle should be the same size with the exception of the "I" which will be only a part of the rectangle and the "M" and "W", wide letters, which will require a rectangle approximately 50% wider than the others. Letters may be cut directly from the paper rectangles or drawn on the paper rectangle first.

Talk about uniform size of letters, spacing between letters within a word, space between words. How is the letter or word affected by the color of the background? Experiment with various color combinations. How may the letters be used? Arranged and pasted on a sheet of colored paper or poster board? Stapled on the bulletin board or set out on large straight pins and pinned to the bulletin board for three-dimensional effect? What other possibilities may be explored to get unusual, attention-getting effects?

This experience may be taken a step further by suggesting single words that have distinctive expressive potential. Have the children form the letters by the cut paper technique and develop appropriate cut or torn paper illustrations to go with the words.

Bulletin board displaying a variety of lettering examples. Two lettering techniques have been combined for the title. The word, "LETTERING", is cut paper letters; the word, "speaks", colored chalk on dark construction paper.

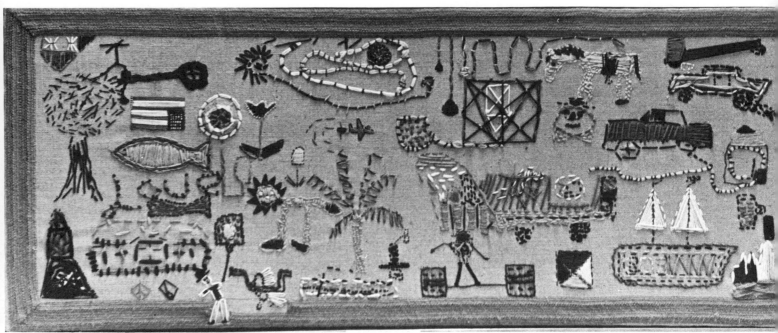

Stitchery mural, age 9.

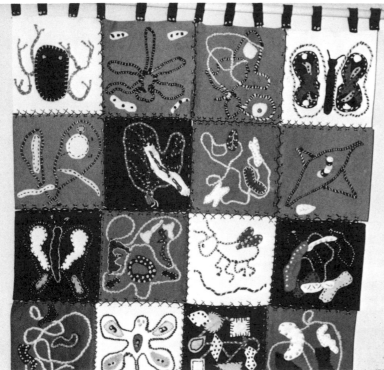

Stitchery wall hanging comprised of several squares of stitched design by individual children, age 9.

F. Saying it with stitches

Tools and materials:
Fabrics — cotton, burlap, different colors of yarn, threads, cord, felt scraps, buttons, trinkets, beads, junk jewelry, needles, scissors.

Emphases:
Using and understanding stitchery techniques as a form of personal expression.
Relating the different kinds of stitches to the design.
Developing skills in stitchery and appliqué.

Activities:
Talk about design and textiles, the ways in which design may be applied to a piece of fabric (printing, dyeing, stitching). How does this differ from weaving where the design is an integral part of the structure of the cloth?

Show examples of stitchery. Have some available for close inspection by the children. Is there a relationship between these designs and designs made by drawing or painting? What can be said with stitches and a piece of cloth? Talk about color, shape, texture, movement, unity of design. Discuss different kinds of stitches: flat, cross, satin, blanket, chain, running, outline. Demonstrate. Have children experiment with thread and scraps of cloth, practicing the making of stitches. Encourage innovation, variation of stitches and use of different colors of thread or yarn.

How can stitches be combined with shapes of cloth to create a design (appliqué)? In what ways can other items (beads, buttons, trinkets) be incorporated into the design to add appeal and interest?

A painting may be framed and displayed on the wall; a clay pot to hold something; a mask to be worn. What can be done with a piece of stitchery? Could it be hung on the wall as a decoration, or made into some type of a container (handbag)? Would it be appropriate as a place mat?

A good follow-up for stitchery experiences would be a weaving activity. This will emphasize the difference between designing *on* cloth and creating a design *in* the cloth. Use box looms or frame looms. Materials would include yarn, cord, string, raffia and other fibers. Clarify the meaning of "warp" and "weft". Demonstrate and let the children take it from there.

Stitchery combined with appliqué, age 9.

Yarn on burlap, stitchery, age 9.

Frame loom.

Weaving in progress on a box loom; fabric being made for a tote purse. Photo courtesy Doris F. Standerfer, Professor of Art and Art Education, San Jose State College, California.

Collage head, age 10.

I. THE WORLD OF THE ARTIST—
People, places, events

Throughout history the artist at different times has made record of people and events, commented on the condition of man, and produced objects to serve his own society. He has built monuments and constructed monumental buildings.

There are countless examples that may be used to support this fact. Select a few such as the following to serve as a basis for classroom discussions: (1) *Ritual masks* of the African primitive artists: unusual patterns and distortions, richly decorated, to serve in ceremonies to secure the favor of the spirits and gain good fortune. (2) *Children's Games* by Pieter Brueghel; a fun-type painting filled with action, excitement, and details of the ordinary 16th century world of the artist. (3) *Liberty Leading the People* by Eugene Delacroix; expression, movement, strong shadows vividly depicting the overthrow of the Bourbon monarch in 1830. (4) *Third Class Carriage* by Honoré Daumier; a record of mid-19th century life in France, the unheroic life of the average man and his plight.

The artists of today influence us through paintings, murals, sculptures in public buildings, and the design of buildings. This discussion may be broadened to go beyond the 20th century painter and sculptor and consider the effect of the fashion designer, the industrial designer and the advertising artist on our lives. Then there is the political cartoonist seen daily in most newspapers commenting on local, national, and world issues of our times. A visit to churches, cathedrals and synagogues in the community would illustrate how art or the work of the artist/craftsman is a significant part of the various services and ceremonies.

Breadline, etching by Reginald Marsh, 1932. Collection the Museum of Modern Art, New York, Abby Aldrich Rockefeller Fund. In this etching Reginald Marsh vividly portrays the plight of man during the depression of the 1930s.

Basket chair, designed by Isama Kenmochi. Collection of the Museum of Modern Art, New York. Gift of Kenmochi Design Associates, Tokyo, Japan.

Ancestral figure, Oceanic, Abelam Tribe, New Guinea. Gift of The Hecht Co., The Baltimore Museum of Art, Baltimore, Maryland.

175

Design for a car of the future — Runabout.
Photo courtesy General Motors Corporation.

Chair, chromed steel and leather, designed by Clement Meadmore, 1963. Collection of the Museum of Modern Art, New York. Gift of David Whitney.

II. OUR ENVIRONMENT—
Products of industry

Products manufactured for daily living in the home and the community are an integral part of the environment. They are made for the purpose of making everyday life more efficient and pleasant and include appliances, furniture, textiles, industrial equipment, systems of transportation — the automobile, buses, airplanes, bicycles. This may be extended to include the profession of graphic design that is characterized by row after row of items on the shelves of supermarkets.

A well-designed bulletin board displaying many different products in the above categories should elicit spontaneous response by the children. Many will eagerly point out those things that they like or dislike. Center the discussion on the diversity of design, use of color, shape of the product in relation to forms, the uncluttered simplicity of good contemporary design.

A trip to a local department store or a presentation by a local designer should be considered when possible. Since awareness of and sensitivity for good design is the fundamental objective of this part of the art program, a creative activity is not always necessary. However, boys are usually interested in drawing, painting, or modeling (wet clay) automobiles; fashions or home decorations have a special appeal to girls.

III. CREATIVE ART ACTIVITIES—

Discuss the relating of art expression to the children's own personal experiences and observations. Can we use painting, sculpture, or printmaking to tell about people we know or have seen, or to describe places we have been? How can visual expression be used to portray school events, or community affairs? Can we relate our visual expression to stories?

Talk about ways in which the art work of the children may have an impact on others — through exhibits in the school: a visual interpretation of a social studies unit, signs and posters, a drawing or painting, matted or framed and prominently displayed at home. Through some of their classroom art experiences the children may design and make objects that have utilitarian value, such as, simple jewelry, a woven scarf or a hooked rug.

Drawing, nylon pen, age 10.

Turtle, wire sculpture.

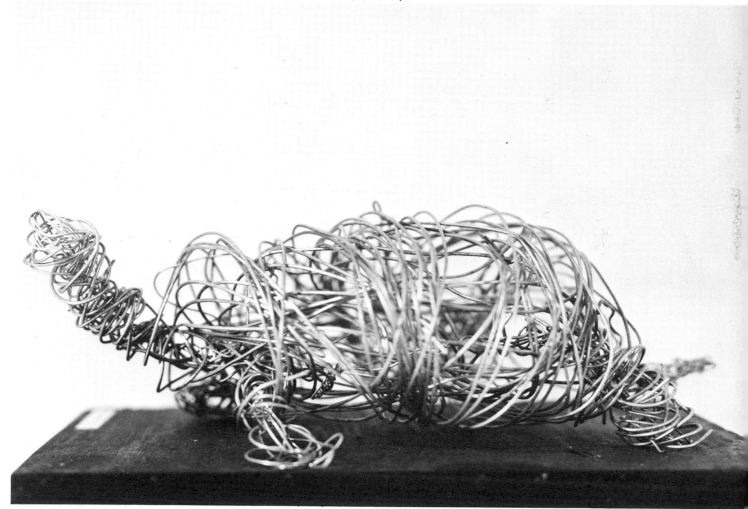

A. Drawing and painting

Tools and materials:

Felt pens, brush and ink, crayons, colored pencils, tempera paints.

Variety of colors, shapes, textures of paper and boards, colored tissue, polyvinyl acetate (white glue thinned with water may be used), brushes, small sponges.

Emphases:

Care and use of drawing and painting tools and materials; control.

Design concepts and visual qualities introduced and learned at previous grade or age level.

Utilization of a variety of techniques (dry brush, overpainting, stippling, blending, combining of materials) in drawing and painting activities.

Creating strong or subtle contrasts through the treatment of line, color, value, texture, shape.

The importance of having something to say in a drawing or painting (figurative or non-figurative, representational or abstract).

The significance of organization, effective composition — center of interest with all other elements related in varying importance; achieving balance, unity, harmony, contrast, simplicity.

Understanding the artist as a recorder of people, places, events.

The influence of the artist-designer on everyday life.

Activities:

Conduct experimental activities related to the art materials suggested for this grade level. Discuss the characteristics of tempera paints. Provide opportunity for the children to discover some additional techniques with tempera paints. Use a loaded brush with one color on dry paper, brushing a second contrasting color into the still wet color on the paper. Wet the paper with a sponge and clean water and apply color with a brush; drip colors on wet paper; intermingle colors. What can be seen in the results? When dry, work over the paper with brush and ink or black tempera, defining shapes that may be either abstract or representative of something familiar. Dampen one

Paints applied on a wet surface.

Collage. Colored tissue and white glue, age 10.

Collage. Yarn and cloth, age 10.

half of the paper with a sponge; place a spot of color on the dry section and by blowing with a straw or tilting the paper move the color into the dampened part of the paper. Make a *wash* — Hold paper at an angle on a drawing board; start at top with a loaded brush and with quick, horizontal strokes, work the color across and down over the surface of the paper. Mix colors to create new colors. Apply to paper. *Stipple, dab, dry brush.* Remove most of the paint from a loaded brush with a towel or cloth, then stroke the brush across the paper. Drag a damp sponge across colors on the paper. What happens? Scrape the dried paint with a knife or pointed tool. Combine tempera paints with other materials such as crayons, wax, felt pens, chalks, black ink.

Using colored tissue, create a series of shapes (different colors) on paper by adhering tissue with PVA or thinned white glue; a thin mixture of wheat paste may also be used . Work over this with felt pen, crayons, tempera paint. Try overlapping colored tissue to create new colors, new shapes. What would result if a piece of colored tissue were balled, dampened in water and pressed against white paper? Does this have application to drawing and painting activities?

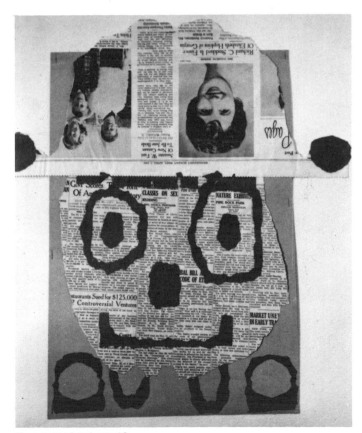

Torn paper head, age 10.

Figure, cut and paste (newspaper), age 10.

Discuss the results of these experimental activities and how they may be adapted to painting problems. In addition to broadening the children's understanding of art materials, this type of experience can often be evaluated in terms of design concepts and strengthen the children's knowledge of color and shape relationships, texture and pattern, developing different kinds of movement, mood, contrast. Frequently, an immediate result is a spontaneous painting.

Understandings and concepts developed through experimental activities should be followed with specific art problems:

Groups of objects

Having had experience in drawing single objects, the sketching or painting of two or more objects presents the new challenge of size and shape relationships, space between objects, overlapping. In addition to found objects (natural and man-made), tools, containers, and materials, that are normally a part of the art program, may be used in this activity. The problem may be extended to include drawing the waste can, sink, water faucets, a cabinet, chair. Suggest drawing the space around and between objects (negative space) rather than the objects themselves. Additional items for this experience may include objects brought from home, musical instruments, scientific equipment used in the school program, athletic equipment. Encourage children to experiment with shape, value, and color and imaginative interpretation. How can items such as these be used to tell a story?

Show examples of art (reproductions) that may motivate children and strengthen organizational concepts, such as *Large Target with Plaster Casts* by Jasper Johns; *Bottle of Red Wine* by Pierre Bonnard; *Still Life* by Paul Cézanne.

Animals and other living creatures

At a very early age children become fascinated by animals, birds, fish, and this interest is often reflected in their graphic expression at all grade levels. In this day of the vanishing horse, children still like to draw horses. This attraction to living creatures cannot be considered unique because even in prehistoric times the cave artists were preoccupied with similar subject matter. Every major period of art has produced its share of animals, birds, and fish in some form.

The children's understanding of the structure and action of living creatures may be developed through observation of household pets, trips to the zoo, the school aquarium. Stuffed animals and birds, when available, make good models. There is always the circus with its lions, tigers, horses, camels, and elephants.

In addition to sketching from direct observation, suggest unusual and imaginary animals, wild colors. Read an interesting, lively story and have the children illustrate it, substituting animals for human characters.

Select pertinent examples of art work (reproductions) such as, *The Sleeping Gypsy* by Henri Rousseau and *The Circus* by Marc Chagall.

Two cut paper renderings of objects; one emphasizing negative space, the other, positive space.

Street scenes

Whether in cities, towns, or villages, the vantage point of the street presents unlimited inspiration for drawing and painting. In previous grade levels it was suggested that children be taken on sketching trips to become perceptive of their environment in general. At this age level, stress selection from and interpretation of the outdoor scene. Take the children on SEEING walks through the streets to observe the many components of the local scene. Observe structure of buildings, textural qualities of various materials, the apparent convergence of lines formed by sidewalks and streets as they disappear in the distance (perspective).

Talk about interest in painting — selection of subject matter, narrowing down the overwhelming scene to a single complete statement. Encourage the children to sketch those points of interest that they would like to paint.

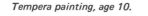
Tempera painting, age 10.

Back in the classroom, review the importance of developing a center of interest in the paintings; achieving balance, unity, and contrast.

Show examples of art (reproductions) that reflect different moods in painting the scene, such as, *The Turning Road* by Paul Cézanne and *Promenade* by Charles Burchfield.

The figure in action

Review general proportions of the figure. Relationships of arms, legs, to each other and to the rest of the body; how and where they bend; how the body moves; angle of the walking or running figure. Discuss different attitudes of the body when performing: jumping, kicking, swinging a baseball bat, skipping. Have the children stand and move, stretch, turn, stoop. Pose one child and have others make quick action sketches, thinking of the total movement of the body rather than details. Suggested materials — large brushes and black ink on classified ad sections of newspaper. Play music that suggests action and have the children interpret in terms of the figure.

Take the children outside to observe and sketch other children on the playground engaging in play activities.

Reproductions of art work by Fernand Léger, Edgar Degas and Ben Shahn should be used to show how different artists interpreted the human figure.

Figure, crayon on newspaper, age 10.

Crayon etching, age 10.

Mural, tempera paint, age 10.

Mural (detail), stitchery, age 10.

Murals

Drawing and painting activities as group projects may be related to other areas of the school program and to community activities in the form of the mural. This kind of experience can bring together all of the art concepts learned through other art activities into a dynamic visual expression on a large scale. Themes may be centered on social studies, health, science, community living and other school-related functions. Group children according to specific roles — selecting theme, researching, planning, materials to be used, executing.

Consideration should be given to those ideas that should be illustrated in the mural to make it a complete statement; relationships of component parts to each other; emphasizing the more important elements; achieving unity of and movement between various parts of the mural; color and size relationships. Materials to be used may be combinations of any art materials that the children have used: tempera paint on kraft paper, chalks, felt pens, inks on long sheets (determined by space in which mural is to be located) of white or colored project paper, cut and torn paper and paste techniques, brushes, sponges, brayers to apply paints to achieve different effects. Another interesting approach is to use yarn, cloth, and threads of different colors to create a fabric mural through stitchery and appliqué techniques. Many additional items such as string, wire, small boxes, wood shapes, and found objects may be used to produce three-dimensional qualities.

Many of the recently constructed office buildings in urban areas have murals usually located on walls in lobby or foyer areas. If this is a possibility, schedule a trip so that the children may have first-hand experience in this kind of project. Show reproductions of art works that have the type of pictorial value associated with murals. Works by Joan Miró and examples, such as, *Guernica* by Pablo Picasso, *Black Trapezium* by Kasimer Malevich and *The Acrobats* by Fernand Legér would be of interest. Also noted for murals is Thomas Hart Benton, 20th century American painter.

B. Linoleum, wood and a print

Tools and materials:

Water soluble inks, various colors and textures of paper, newspaper.

Unmounted linoleum, pieces of soft wood (white pine), heavy grained pieces of wood.

Linoleum cutting gauges, stencil knives, brayers, ink slabs (glass or formica).

Emphases:

Developing concepts of line to define shape and to create textures and patterns.

Extending the understanding of printing from raised surfaces.

Discovering textures in the process of using grainy wood, textured paper, inks.

185

Linoleum print combined with colored chalks, age 10.

Repeat print, age 10.

Print on newspaper, age 10.

Activities:

Provide time for the children to become familiar with tools and materials to be used. Small scraps of linoleum and soft wood should be made available to practice the handling of gauges and stencil knives. Demonstrate proper use of tools particularly the cutting away from hands to avoid injury.

Set up inking stations (brayers, inks, ink slabs) so that the children can make prints from the scraps on which they have been experimenting. Talk about the results. What part of the block makes the print? What happens when ink is rolled on a piece of grainy, textured wood and then printed on paper? How can these experiments be used in making a print? By this time some of the children may have discovered that the print made from a block is the reverse of the block; also that lines or shapes cut into the linoleum or wood do not print but that part of the surface that remains, prints.

Discuss the potential of blockprinting as a means for expressing an idea. How does this relate to drawing and painting? How does it differ? What subject matter or themes would be appropriate for this form of visual expression? What are the limitations in telling a story with a print?

Talk about the block print as a means for duplicating a design many times.

Emphasizing the importance of the idea, suggest the making of preliminary sketches for the print. After the children have organized their ideas and determined their designs, point out again the need for reversing their drawings when transferring them to the linoleum or wood block. The children should be able to take it from here.

After cutting their designs into the blocks, the children should pull proofs by inking the blocks and pressuring paper against them. Encourage them to experiment with different combinations of colored inks and papers. Make prints on newspaper pages and magazines. Try overprints: print with one color then use the same block and print over it with another color. Overprinting is more effective when the second print is offset a bit from the first.

Show examples of prints by artists such as, Paul Gauguin, Kathe Kollwitz, Antonio Frasconi and Leonard Baskin.

Linoleum print, age 10.

Slab-built tray.

Slab-constructed sculpture.

C. A clay slab

Tools and materials:

Wet clay, tables protected by oilcloth or newspapers.

Rolling pins, wood strips approximately one-quarter of an inch thick and twelve to eighteen inches long, paring knives.

Emphases:

Understanding the potential of a clay slab as a basis for creative expression.

Developing skill in the use of clay.

Developing concepts of shape, form and texture as they relate to clay.

Activities:

Making a clay slab of uniform thickness is a relatively simple activity. Place a ball of wet clay on the covered table, between two wood strips of equal thickness. Press the clay down with the hands, then roll out with a rolling pin.

Now that you have a large flat slab of clay what can you do with it? Would it be possible to draw a design on the surface of the slab? Try a thin stick, a toothpick, a nail. Suggest cutting into the clay (similar to cutting a linoleum block), adding clay to the surface, pressing objects (jar lids, dowels, gears, large-head nails) into the clay slab to create patterns and textures.

If the slab were cut into rectangular shapes, could these be joined together to make a container, or to make a figure or animal, or just an interesting three-dimensional form?

Textures produced by pressing various objects into clay.

Slab-built relief sculpture.

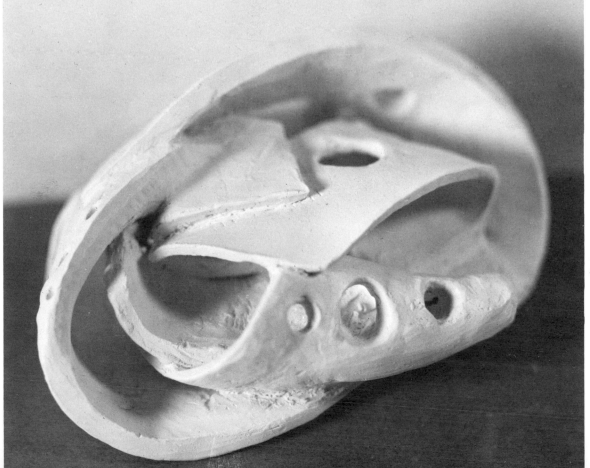

Slab-built sculptural form.

Some of the children may be interested in a technique whereby they can duplicate a design in clay, producing a number of clay tiles of the same design. Start with a square or rectangle (5″ by 5″, 4″ by 6″) cut from the slab. Develop the desired design on this shape, using any of the techniques discussed here. Place the completed design in a cardboard box, allowing some space around the edges. Pour plaster of Paris over this to a thickness at least one inch greater than that of the clay design. The plaster will harden. Remove it from the box and take away the clay used to make the original design. You now have a master mold that should be referred to as a *press mold* since duplicate designs may be made by pressing soft clay into the mold. How can a set of tiles, formed by this method, be used?

Suggest cutting one large shape (oval, circle, square, rectangle, free-form) out of a slab. Have the children drape the shapes over forms (side of a large cylindrical container, a large ball, newspaper crumpled tightly into a rounded form). What happens? Place similar slabs on pieces of cloth and hang like a hammock. This may be done by attaching cloth over the end of an open box. When the clay slab is placed on the cloth it will sag and shape the clay. How can these new forms be used? Do they suggest bowls? Trays? Masks?

Of equal importance to the making of a clay form is the decorating of the surface of the finished product. When the clay is still in plastic form, the surface may be changed by cutting or scratching into, adding on, or texturing with various objects mentioned earlier. Clay objects, dried to room temperature or preferably bisque-fired, may also be decorated with underglazes and glazes. Provide opportunity for children to use various underglaze and glaze colors to decorate their clay products. How does the color enhance? Should a solid color be used to cover the entire surface, or does the object suggest the use of several colors?

Experiment

Follow-up activities may include carving into blocks of leather-hard clay, or into blocks of plaster formed by pouring plaster mixed with sand or vermiculite into empty milk cartons.

Tray shape, formed by draping slab over a ball.

Basic shape formed by joining two slabs around three cardboard tubes.

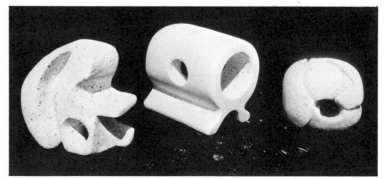

Three forms carved from plaster blocks.

D. Paper, pulp, and—

Tools and materials:

A pile of old newspapers, buckets or large plastic mixing bowls, wheat paste, paints, brushes and many odds and ends such as cloth, yarn, string, buttons, beads.

Emphases:

Exploring the possibilities of paper as a modeling material.

Developing three-dimensional design concepts with a plastic material.

Activities:

Although modeling with paper pulp is an experience somewhat similar to working with clay and other plastic compounds, its uniqueness is that the children will be involved in making their own basic material for use in building an art form. Then too, this is an activity in which the essential ingredient (newspaper) is generally accepted as a discard.

The pulp is made by tearing old newspapers into very small pieces, soaking these pieces in water, squeezing the water out and adding wheat paste. All that is needed now are the hands and imaginations of the children.

Imaginative bird with coat hanger wire feet.

Modeling a mask with pulp.

Discuss other uses for paper pulp as an art material, such as masks and paper jewelry. Bracelets may be made by bending a strip of cardboard into a loop and developing a design on the surface with paper pulp. Strips of colored tissue may be wrapped around this to produce interesting color combinations. Use wheat paste or thinned white glue to adhere the colored tissue.

Handling the material itself may be sufficient motivation to start young minds working. Is paper pulp a good material for modeling a figure, or a creature of fantasy? Further discussion with the children as they experiment with the pulp should bring out additional creative ideas.

Another kind of stimulation could evolve from a social studies unit, a story, a play, or a song. An important event in history can take on new meaning through a diorama containing lively figures made from paper pulp. Perhaps some of the children would be interested in making puppets for a play. Have them form the puppet heads by building and shaping with paper pulp on the end of a piece of cardboard tubing. Puppet heads may also be made by modeling pulp over worn-out electric bulbs.

Talk about the finishing of objects made with paper pulp. Can they be painted? How can other materials be used effectively: yarn for hair, cloth, buttons, beads?

Diorama. Pulp and other materials, age 10.

"Gulliver". Combination of papier-mâché and paper pulp, age 10.

Pulp and other materials, age 10.

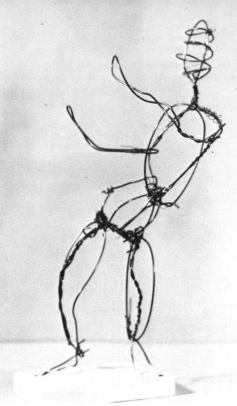

Drawing with wire in space.

E. Space and constructing

Tools and materials:

Soft wires: copper, aluminum, stovepipe, bell wire, telephone wire; wire cutters.

Balsa wood strips (1/8"), applicator sticks, fast-drying glue.

Emphases:

Using three-dimensional line to express an idea.

Developing concepts of space as an integral part of design.

Achieving action, movement, and spirit in three-dimensional forms.

Activities:

Two sets of materials are suggested for constructing experiences. Divide the class into two parts, assigning one set of materials to each group. This will provide a broader base for discussion when evaluating the activity.

In the first group, soft wire, the basic material, has engaging qualities and great potential. Put a piece of soft copper wire in the hands of almost anyone and watch what happens! Provide opportunity for the children to experiment with lengths of wire. Suggest bending the wire, drawing in space, coiling to produce springy effects, balling to create mass and volume.

Talk about the interpretation of an idea with wire. Suggest ways in which action can be expressed: a figure running, jumping, kicking, throwing, a bird in flight, a fish, bug, butterfly. Discuss the importance of the action or spirit of the idea rather than minute details; linear effects, open space. What other materials may be used to enhance the wire form? How can this activity be related to school and community activities?

Wire figures with emphasis on mass.

Materials for the second group may be more closely associated with architectural structures and non-objective sculpture. Show examples such as, Buckminster Fuller's *Geodesic Dome* and the work of Naum Gabo, Antoine Pevsner, Richard Lippold, Maholy-Nagy; George Rickey's *Four Lines Up* is quite appropriate. Talk about the linear qualities of balsa wood strips, applicator sticks, vertical or horizontal directional characteristics, the creating of interest by designing with a series of repeated shapes (triangles, squares, rectangles).

Follow-up activities may involve the children in designing with cardboard shapes, or constructing a sculptural form by joining a number of similar shapes into one unit (slotting and joining or gluing). Wire forms may be transformed into new images by dripping wet plaster over the wire, or by adding strips of cloth dipped in wet plaster. Another interesting spin-off would be studying various found or junk objects: gears, nuts, bolts, nails, discarded kitchen utensils, or wood scraps and seeking relationships of such materials to young ideas.

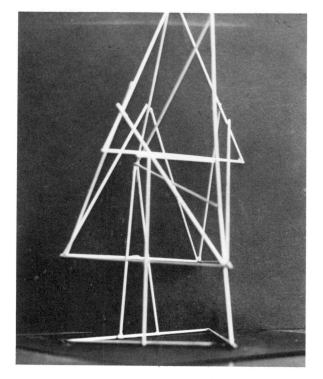

Space structure with strong vertical direction.

Cardboard shapes added to produce solid areas of interest.

F. Signs of the times

Tools and materials:

Various colors of paper, poster board, paste, tempera paints, transparent watercolors, brushes, scissors.

Emphases:

Developing skill in lettering; uniformity, spacing, readability.

Understanding the importance of visual impact in promoting an idea or event.

Applying an art skill to a practical situation.

Activities:

At a previous grade level the children were introduced to a simple cut paper technique for lettering. Review this.

Discuss the wide use of signs in various parts of community and school life. Signs that give direction, signs that announce events, informational signs, humorous signs. Display pertinent materials on the bulletin board. In addition to commercial signs that may be available, some newspaper and magazine ads and folders (particularly travel folders) are quite effective as a basis for motivation and classroom discussion. How does the lettering reflect the specific message? How does the lettering relate to the illustration or symbol being used? In what way does color express the feeling of the idea?

Talk about ways in which the children may combine cut paper letters with symbols or simple illustrations to present a point in a dynamic, forceful, visual way. Emphasize simplicity. These signs may be related to school events or to community-oriented topics (Better Health, Safety, Clean-up the Neighborhood).

A similar activity to develop the children's understandings of the graphic image and visual impact may be through their expressive interpretation of words such as, *fire, war, peace, transportation, speed, outer space, brotherhood.* Another source of themes for this project may center on the children's personal ideas regarding what they hope to be: *nurse, fireman, policeman, doctor, scientist, astronaut.* How can these words be illustrated?

Individual projects should be completed on poster board, using cut paper letters in combination with cut paper or painted illustrations or symbols.

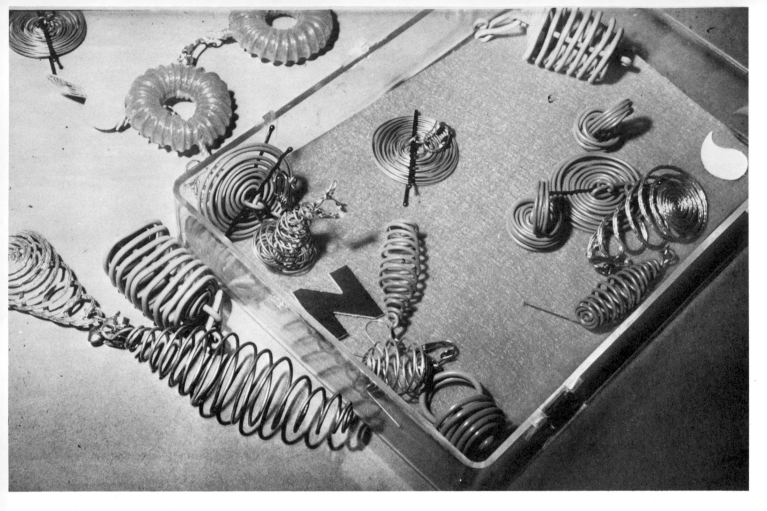

G. Personal adornment

Tools and materials:

Various kinds of soft wire including copper, stove-pipe, aluminum. Bell wire and wire used by telephone companies are covered with brightly colored insulation (reds, greens, blues, yellows) that makes them popular for wire jewelry; jewelry findings.

Beads, discarded costume jewelry parts, wire cutters.

Emphases:

Broadening concepts of line in three-dimensional form as an element of design.

Understanding design as it relates to a decorative and functional object.

Developing skills in a creative craft area.

Activities:

Throughout history, man has directed considerable effort toward personal adornment. Primitive tribes used this art form in conjunction with ceremonial activities. In ancient Egypt jewelry was a symbol of the life style of the kingdom or dynasty. The many civilizations that followed considered jewelry as an important element in social life, often as a sign of affluence. Today jewelry in many forms is common to all walks of life.

Have the children examine wire in terms of its potential as a basic material for making jewelry. Would it be appropriate for earrings, pendants, bracelets, necklaces? How can wire be adapted to such forms of jewelry? Show examples of contemporary jewelry. Suggest coiling the wire around dowels of various sizes; around other forms. After the dowels or forms have been removed note that the wire coil now has a spring-like shape. Stretch it. What can be done with this to transform it into a specific piece of jewelry? Another technique would be to work flat on the table, coiling the wire in a manner similar to a watch spring. Could the results of these two techniques be combined to fashion a necklace? Provide time for the children to experiment by bending, twisting several strands, coiling, joining wire, and adding beads and parts from discarded costume jewelry. These materials combined with young, inventive minds should produce fascinating results.

H. Rugs and other things

Tools and materials:

These should be organized according to the specific craft activity (See bibliography).

Emphases:

Exploring ideas and developing design concepts as they relate to personal crafts experiences.

Applying understandings of line, shape, color, and texture to crafts activities. Stress simplicity of design and visual order.

Developing proficiency in the use of crafts materials, techniques, and processes; good craftsmanship.

Activities:

Crafts experiences usually generate an unparalleled enthusiasm among children. Perhaps this is due to the excitement of handling the many kinds of materials associated with crafts; or the enchantment of the different techniques and processes utilized in converting material into a functional product. Nevertheless, who can overlook the thrill and satisfaction that a child senses when he has completed his own hooked rug, woven scarf, dyed place mat, or piece of cloth containing an original repeat design?

Woven handbag.

Hooked rug.

Stitchery.

It is suggested that crafts projects related to textiles should be programmed for children at this grade level. These may include rug hooking or knotting, weaving on box or frame looms, the inkle loom, two harness table loom, tie and dye designs on cloth, an additional stitchery technique such as drawn work, and creating repeat designs on cloth with stencils.

Space will not allow a full description of each of these crafts processes. However, several publications included in the bibliography of this book deal specifically with these areas of creative expression. An outstanding book containing excellent photographs and simple, direct descriptions of most crafts areas is *Crafts Design* by Moseley, Johnson, and Koenig, Wadsworth Publishing Co., Belmont, California.

Products that would be of interest to children designing in various textile areas would include small rugs, scarves, handbags, ties, pot holders, place mats, samplers, wall hangings, room dividers, designs on cloth to be made into an article of clothing.

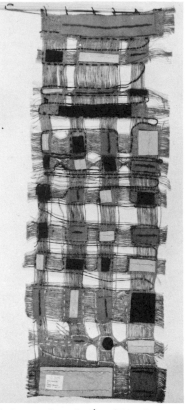

Wall hanging.

Children working on stitchery and appliqué wall hanging.

Street scene, colored chalks, age 11.

I. THE WORLD OF THE ARTIST—
Styles of expression

The study of art is a study of contrasts. The same idea, the same subject, the same structure has been expressed in divergent ways. The 20th century in particular has been a period of many contrasts in the way in which the artist has expressed himself.

This may be illustrated by showing good reproductions of art from the various movements of the 20th century (Cubism, Dadaism, Surrealism, Abstract-Expressionism, Pop, Op, and other trends of the '60s) and relating them to art of past cultures.

The discussion may center on specific subject matter such as, *Woman on a Bicycle* by Willem de Kooning; *American Gothic* by Grant Wood; *The Green Violinist* by Marc Chagall; *The Seated Clown* by Georges Roualt; *Girl Before a Mirror* by Pablo Picasso. These paintings vividly illustrate different styles of artists in their interpretation of subject matter. The balanced composition, *Italian Comedians* by Antoine Watteau, early 18th century, may be contrasted with the moving, colorful, angular forms in *Mardi Gras* by Paul Cézanne, late in the 19th century.

Discuss the different ways in which artists used line, color, and texture to visualize subject matter. In what way does one composition vary from another? Is detail of equal importance to each artist? How is feeling or mood expressed?

How does this relate to the work of the child as he creates? Is realism the only answer in child art? How can a feeling for movement, action, and the spirit of an idea be expressed? Is personal style important to the child?

Christ Mocked by the Soldiers. Georges Roualt, collection of the Museum of Modern Art, New York, given anonymously.

II. OUR ENVIRONMENT—
The changing scene, urban and rural

The size of organized communities ranges from the small rural towns to vast metropolitan areas. Today, regardless of size, problems of transportation, deterioration, and overcrowding are common to all.

The work of urban or town planners is to create a more efficient and visually appealing organization of streets, land, buildings, landmarks; to remove pollution, congestion, depletion of natural resources, and general deterioration. In many communities there are exciting and refreshing examples of urban renewal and preservation: pleasant shopping malls, new green areas and parks, recreational facilities and new buildings to replace and revitalize slum areas. Good examples to illustrate this may be drawn from cities and towns across the country: central business districts in Baltimore, Dallas, San Francisco; the United Nations complex in New York City. Then there are new cities such as Reston, Virginia and Columbia, Maryland that are exciting adventures in designing for quality living.

What causes a town or city to be attractive as opposed to disorderly and ugly? Is the local community concerned about its appearance? What evidences are there of revitalization (new buildings, refurbished store fronts, green areas, control of signs)? What factors produce a slum area? How has industry changed (industrial parks, relocating)?

Invite local officials, city planners, architects, engineers, in to discuss their role in improving the local community.

Take the children into the community to observe the ugly spots as well as renewed areas. There are many classroom activities that may grow out of this experience: (1) Redesign a store front. (2) Sketch areas of deterioration and plan improvements. (3) Design a poster promoting local interest in a litter-free, clean community. (4) Design a small park. (5) Design a piece of sculpture for the park.

Part of downtown San Antonio River after beautification.

III.   CREATIVE ART ACTIVITIES

Although the entire elementary school art program is designed to encourage a creative response by the children, a particular emphasis at this level should be directed toward the importance of personal style. Whether the children are involved in painting, making a print, constructing a three-dimensional form, or engaged in some other type of visual expression, the ultimate sense of satisfaction or achievement should be highly individualistic. Some groups or activities may be programmed to include selection by the child of specific materials and art processes for the visualizing of an idea.

In discussing personal style refer to the divergency of expression as seen, principally, in the works of 20th century artists. Point out the range from realism, and a concern for detailed representation to examples of art in which there is no apparent attempt to identify with subject matter. Then talk about the child's approach to visual expression. Does everybody see the same thing or respond to similar experiences in the same way? How can we express our feelings with color, create interest through nonobjective form, interpret movement, action and the spirit of an idea with materials? Music and recorded sounds (sources unknown to the children) may be used in experimental activities with art materials to extend the children's concepts of personal visual expression.

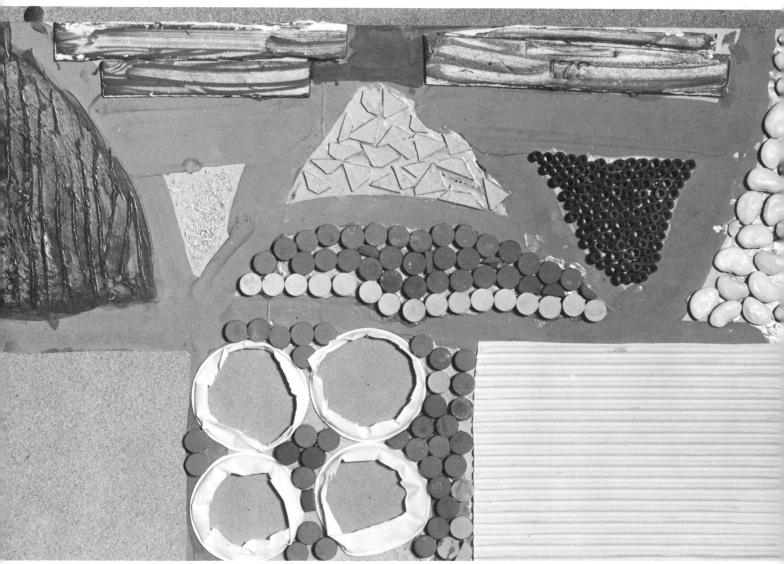

Collage. Corrugated cardboard, cork, tempera paint, sawdust and other materials, age 11.

A. Drawing, painting

Tools and materials:

Felt pens, ball-point pens, colored inks, charcoal, crayon, tempera paint, colored tissue and PVA (polyvinyl acetate).

Assorted papers and boards of various colors and textures (colored poster board, pebble board, newsprint, construction paper, corrugated board, found materials.

Brushes, pens (straight points, lettering), sticks and twigs that may be used with inks, scissors, stencil knives, glue and paste.

Emphases:

Care and control of drawing and painting materials.

New techniques and potential of materials used for self-expression.

Unlimited sources of ideas for drawing and painting in nature and man-made forms (environment).

Interpretation and personal style of expression — capturing the feeling or mood; symbolism, distortion, invention; realism in contrast with nonrepresentational form.

Importance of composition (picture organization) and design.

Utilizing direct experiences in the environment as bases for graphic expression.

The artist, his personal life, and relationship of his art to the society in which he lived.

Activities:

Continue activities that allow children to study materials, to search out new ways to use them in their art expression. Demonstration and discussion will inspire children to higher levels of achievement through experimentation.

One concept that may be emphasized at this age level is the utilization of materials that are generally thought of as being flat (cardboard, paper, cloth) to produce three-dimensional qualities in drawing and painting. Building up the surface by cutting and gluing shapes cut from cardboard or corrugated board may produce a *figurative* as well as a *nonobjective* or *nonrepresentational* composition, depending upon the intent or choice of the child. Talk about the various effects that may be achieved through this technique. What other materials may be used to create three-dimensional qualities in painting? For example, found objects, wood scraps, textured materials, small cardboard boxes assembled on a stiff background. Discuss the relationship of this experience to collage which originally meant the organizing of a design through the cutting or tearing of paper, cardboard, cloth and pasting these parts into desired positions to create a design.

Further experimentation may be conducted in the completing of these three-dimensional paintings such as: (1) painting the entire surface a single color, emphasizing the play of light on the surface and the shadows developed by recessed areas, (2) the use of color on the raised surfaces to achieve a feeling of movement or to show detail, (3) the pasting of contrasting shapes of colored tissue over and around the surface forms.

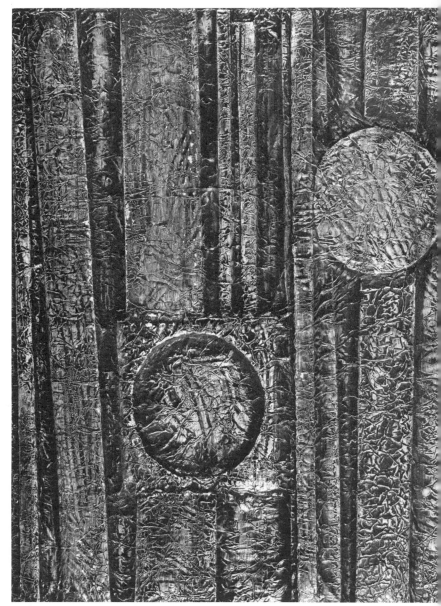

Surface built up with cardboard shapes, covered with aluminum foil and tinted with tempera paints.

Abstract design, corrugated cardboard, age 11.

Keeping in mind that children at this age level have been involved in many painting activities for several years and are generally acquainted with traditional materials, the introduction of techniques that are new to them has a tremendous motivational effect on them. At the same time this approach will assist in the broadening of their concepts of design and of the diversity that has characterized much of the art of this century. Textural qualities may be explored by mixing sand in tempera paint, painting on corrugated board, painting on wood, incorporating fabrics into parts of the design. Crayons melted in muffin tins may be applied to the painting surface with stiff bristle brushes or sticks, or dripped on the surface. Technically this is referred to as *encaustic.*

Other experimental suggestions: (1) crayon drawing on wood shapes or blocks, (2) painting on the surfaces of boxes — a single box or more to form a unit, (3) colored inks or colored felt pens on acetate and projecting the design with an overhead projector, (4) inks, felt pens, colored tissue on 2″ x 2″ glass to produce slides.

Tempera-ink resist is another painting technique that has great appeal to children. Upon the completion of the tempera painting, the entire design is coated with black ink. After this dries, the paper is placed in a sink and washed with a gentle flow of water from the faucet. The unexpected!

Portrait. Colored tissue, felt, burlap, yarn and tempera, age 11.

String design, age 11.

Mural, cut paper, age 11.

Drawing and painting activities:

In previous grades the children have had experiences in drawing objects, figures, and animals and should have some basic understanding of proportion, action, texture, and color as they relate to this kind of subject matter. Some attention should be given (as the situation dictates) to a general review of these areas. However, greater concentration should be placed upon the whole approach to drawing and painting and the development of compositional concepts in the expressing of an idea. Although it may still be convenient to organize drawing and painting activities around subject matter such as a figure, self-portraits or portraits, objects, cityscapes and landscapes, of greater importance is the development of personal style, creative vitality, perceptual awareness, and the general ability to use materials in a creative way.

Topics or themes for drawing and painting experiences should be related to the specific interests of the children. The range is broad and includes: the personal experiences of the child (home, school, community), holidays, seasons, events of history and of today, the world, the universe, natural phenomena, communications, transportation, industry, imagination, fantasy, "surprise me", color, line, shape, texture. Also, express or suggest something that is related to music, sound, light, movement, smell, touch. Examination of natural objects such as seeds, shells, flowers, fruits, vegetables, and seedpods.

Present examples (films, filmstrips, reproductions) of art works that represent some of the variety of art movements of the 20th century, such as:

(1) *Cubism* during the first part of the century — Picasso, Braque. Traditional perspective gave way to nonrepresentational form, interlocking planes, several views of the same object or figure at the same time.

(2) *Dadaism* and anti-art; the rebellion against "pure" art. The Dadaists were inventive, incisive, sarcastic, and questioned the true function or value of art. Duchamp, Arp, Schwitters.

(3) *Surrealism* and the influence of psychoanalysis; the exploring of the subconscious and the dream world. Dali, Magritte, Miró.

(4) *Abstract Expressionism* — Mondrian, Kandinsky, Pollock, De Kooning.

(5) The 1960s: Op Art — Poons, Anuszkiewicz; *Pop* and Andy Warhol, Claes Oldenburg, Robert Indiana; Minimal, devoid of content, subject-less — Donald Judd, Tony Smith, Robert Morris; Hard-edge, Ellsworth Kelly.

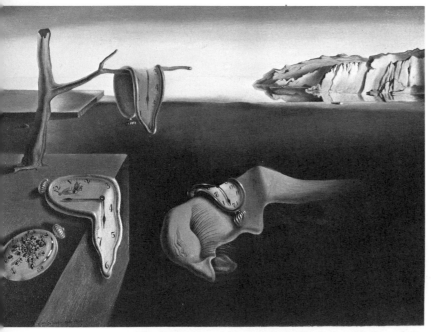

The Persistence of Memory, Salvador Dali, collection of the Museum of Modern Art, New York, given anonymously.

Figure, tempera paint, age 11.

Zebras, watercolor, age 11.

Portrait, charcoal. age 11.

Print, silk screen, torn paper shapes for block-out.

B. Silk, a stencil and a print
Tools and materials:

Silk (organdy may be used) stretched over a cardboard or wood frame, tape, stapler, water-base silk-screen paint or tempera paint mixed with liquid starch, crayons, glue, lacquer, drawing paper, colored construction paper, newsprint, scissors.

Emphases:

Understanding the silk-screen stencil process as a means for creative expression.

Developing skill in a process whereby a design may be duplicated.

Applying design concepts and ideas to an additional printmaking technique.

Activities:

Silk-screen printing is essentially the technique of printing a design through cloth (silk or organdy) that has been stretched on a frame. In some respects this is similar to earlier experiences the children may have had with stencil printing.

Commercially and professionally, silk-screen printing equipment can be quite sophisticated, ranging from shaped screens used to print labels on bottles to photographically prepared screens. However, the techniques suggested here are simplified yet with sufficient interest and depth for the child at this age level.

The primary piece of equipment is the *printing frame.* This may be made in a number of ways:

1 — Cut the center portion out of the lid of a cardboard gift or shoe box. Leave approximately a one inch margin all around to give the frame strength. Staple the cloth (silk or organdy) tightly to the frame and it is ready for use.

2 — Make a frame (some picture frames are suitable) out of 1'' x 1'' wood strips and staple cloth to it.

3 — Small screens, made by stretching cloth across embroidery hoops, are very effective.

After constructing the frame, the activity becomes one of design and of method for transposing the design to the printing frame. Point out to the children that paint will go through the cloth on the printing frame and in order to produce a design some method for blocking out portions of the cloth must be used. Areas where the cloth is blocked out will prevent paint from passing through and consequently print a design. How can this be accomplished? Discuss and demonstrate or have the children explore various possibilities:

1 — Cut a design out of paper. Place on a pad of old newspapers. Center the *printing frame* over this; pour a quantity of paint at one end. Using a squeegee (small window squeegee; piece of heavy cardboard) pull the paint across the entire screen. Now lift the screen and you will see the print on the top of the newspaper pad. You will also notice that the cut paper design has been adhered to the screen. The screen is ready to produce a number of prints by placing it on clean paper and pulling the paint across it.

2 — Draw a design on paper. Place this design beneath the printing frame. Using a wax crayon, trace the design onto the screen. Some areas may be crayoned solid. What is happening? How will this print? Try it! Place the printing frame on a piece of plain paper,

add paint at one end, squeegee across and —? Crayon may be removed from the cloth with benzine solvent.

3 — Draw or paint the design on the cloth with lacquer or thinned waterproof glue. Make a print after the glue or lacquer has dried thoroughly.

Are there other ways that could be explored for blocking out a design on the cloth screen? How do the results of the three methods described above differ?

Have the children experiment with various color combinations, paint and paper: making a repeat design, using the screen process for making a sign, cutting shapes from gummed paper or tape to form a design on the screen, using cut paper letters in combination with the screen to duplicate a sign.

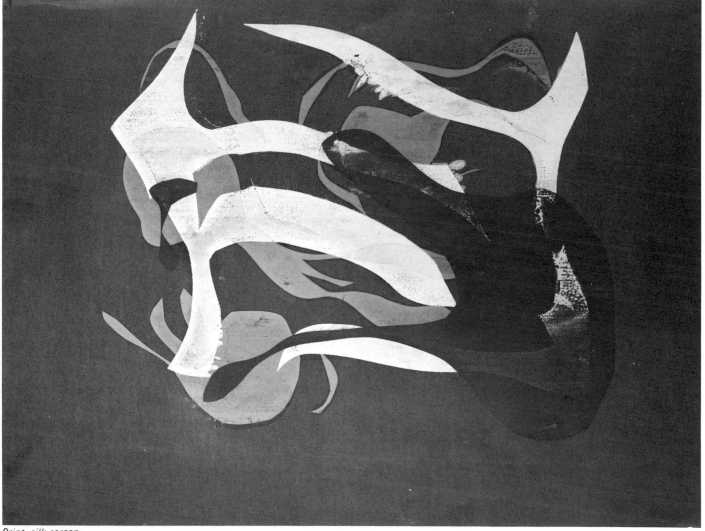

Print, silk screen.

Printmaking offers many opportunities for the child's inventive nature. Since most of the children at this level have had an assortment of printmaking activities, ranging from scrap to cardboard, textured objects, string, brayer, monoprinting and others, open the involvement up to their imaginations. They will have fun in expanding their concepts of duplicating designs, and so will the teacher! Experiences may be extended to combine the silk-screen method with printmaking processes such as those mentioned above. What kind of an effect would result by overprinting a silk-screen print, containing a number of colorful shapes, with the linear qualities of a string print, or the textural qualities produced by the grain of a piece of weathered wood? Try transforming a screen print into an entirely new design by working over it with felt pens or brush and paint.

Print, linoleum, age 11.

Print, found objects, age 11.

Repeat design, print, styrofoam, age 11.

C. Clay and various directions

Tools and materials:
Wet clay, protection for the tables (newspaper, oil cloth), sticks, gears and other found objects, paring knives, rolling pins and wood strips.
Maturing fingers, hands and ideas.

Emphases:
Shaping new and personal concepts of three-dimensional design in clay.

Combining previously learned techniques to make new forms.

Developing skill in the use of clay as a material for visual expression.

Activities:
At earlier age levels the children have used clay — pushing, pulling, pinching, splitting and joining it. They have discovered the clay coil and the slab techniques. Quite possibly they have had some time to carve into a block of clay or to make a plaster mold and press clay into it to produce an exciting

relief form. They have used glazes and underglazes to decorate the surfaces of clay objects. Thus, the eleven-year-old child should have a rather thorough understanding of clay as a plastic material that will bend to his will as he associates a specific idea with it. However, a quick review of past experiences will strengthen the present base for continuing activities with clay. Such a review should be conducted with clay available to the children.

Since personal style in visual expression is an important part of the program at this age level, the children should be encouraged to relate their ideas to the material, using those techniques that will be most helpful in the production of specific ideas. This will differ from clay activities in previous grades when, for example, the exploration was based upon a single technique such as, coil construction. Therefore, one child may combine slab, coil and pinch pot techniques in forming a figure or an animal while another may favor the additive method: adding and modeling clay to build a desired form.

Discuss with the children their interests and ideas in terms of the material, clay. This should result in a variety of directions, from figures to animals, groups of figures and crazy animals, relief designs, nonobjective structures, masks, functional forms including bowls, pots, trays.

Talk about the possible use of clay to design a mosaic. Two approaches may be considered. (1) Start with small balls of clay ½″ to ¾″ in diameter. Flatten these with hands or a rolling pin for a smooth surface. Try gears, ends of dowels that have been carved, corrugated cardboard, and other objects pressed into the clay balls to produce flattened but textured shapes (tiles). Glazes may be added to produce color. The mosaic design will be determined by how these fired, disc-like tiles are assembled and glued to a solid surface. This may move into another direction and become a ceramic jewelry activity. (2) Roll out a slab of clay. Using a paring knife, cut the slab into tiles. These may be somewhat uniform in shape or, if desired, cut into irregular shapes of different sizes. Discuss ways in which the surface of individual tiles may be modified to create interest in the design. Glaze, fire, and assemble into a mosaic design.

The pinch pot, often relegated to the very young child, can become a rather sophisticated approach to design. How can several pinch pot shapes be organized into a unified sculptural form? Explore pinch pots as a technique for making imaginative creatures, fantasy people.

Encourage a free wheeling approach. Show many examples of clay products through films, slides, reproductions. A child should have time to experiment, to use many different techniques, to shape and re-shape his clay. Everything made does not have to be fired. Ultimately his search will lead to a satisfying experience and reflect his concepts and understandings of design as they relate to this specific three-dimensional experience.

Fish, ceramic, age 11.

D. Paper, wood, wire and—form

Additional study of form, representational or non-representational, should be conducted with a variety of plastic and nonplastic materials being made available to the children. Those materials suggested here are familiar to the children, having been used by them in many previous art experiences (paper for painting, printmaking, mâché etc.; wood for construction, printmaking, etc.; wire for sculpture). This part of the art program may be implemented through discussion of how paper, wood and wire may be combined to create three-dimensional forms, providing the children an opportunity to study the materials in relation to a specific idea: figures, animals, space structures. On the other hand, it may be desirable to organize the materials into separate groups to suggest experiences that are definitive.

Tools and materials:

Paper sculpture: Various kinds and weights of paper (drawing, colored construction, metallic, tag board, poster board), scissors, cutting knives, cutting boards (12" x 12" plywood), stapler, tape, pins.

Wood carving: Soft wood blocks (white pine), cutting knives, gouges.

Mobiles: stovepipe wire, aluminum or copper wire, cardboard, heavy colored paper (cover stock), nylon thread, tempera paints, brushes, scissors, cutting knives, wire cutters, round nose pliers.

Emphases:

Although the above groupings of tools and materials suggest three different art activities, the common emphasis is on expressing an idea in three-dimensional form. Paper sculpture and mobiles are constructing experiences in which materials are brought together into a unified design; wood carving involves the children in cutting away, subtracting from a material to shape an idea. Additional emphases would include relating design concepts to materials and ideas and developing specific skills and good craftsmanship.

Paper sculpture

Discuss some of the ways by which paper may be changed from a flat surface into a sculptural form. Have the children experiment by folding, rolling, and stapling to produce a cylinder; cutting into the center of a round piece of paper, and stapling, to make a cone shape; fringing by cutting into the edge of a strip of paper by pulling it between the thumb and a straightedge; scoring (pulling a dull edge such as the back of a scissor blade across the paper) to make a variety of folds. How can these techniques be used to construct a mask, a figure, an animal? Discuss ways by which paper may be joined including pasting, stapling, taping, cutting and slotting.

Wood carving

Show examples of relief sculpture and sculpture in-the-round. Talk about design in relation to a block of wood; carving the design into the flat surface of the wood. Is there some similarity here to cutting a linoleum block, carving into plaster or a slab of clay? How does this differ from carving into all sides of the block? Discuss the differences between relief carving and sculpture in-the-round. Relief or raised carving is viewed primarily from a flat surface; sculpture in-the-round may be viewed from all angles. Carved pieces may be finished by sanding the surface or by rough-texturing it. Oils or liquid waxes with pigments added may also be considered for a different type of finish.

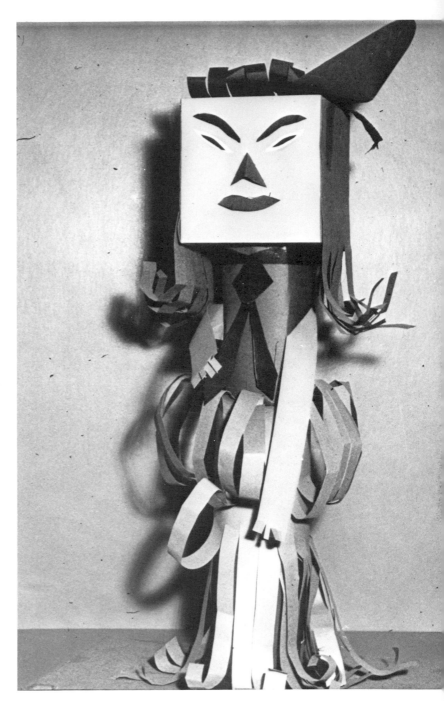

Relief mask, wood.

Mobiles

The term "mobile" has been often misinterpreted as almost any kind of a shape or structure that is designed to be hung on a string. A true mobile should be balanced so that it turns and moves freely. Show examples of mobile sculpture by Alexander Calder.

In addition to movement and balance, two dominant characteristics of mobiles are shape and line. Suggest simple basic shapes, such as circles, rectangles, free forms and slightly curved wire arms to which the shapes will be attached. The mobile is assembled from the bottom up. Locate the center of balance for the bottom arm. Wire the shape(s) in place by tying a length of thread to the approximate center and moving it, as necessary, to balance. Attach this to the end of the next wire arm and locate the center of balance for the second wire arm in a similar way. This procedure should be repeated until the entire mobile is assembled. Note how movement and action become a natural part of the completed mobile sculpture. Talk about color, shape and line and the interplay of these elements in the ever-changing design of the mobile. Discuss other ways to assemble the components of a mobile. How can other effects be achieved by linking together a number of similar shapes with thread? Could the wire arms of a mobile be joined directly by forming loops in the arms at the center of balance and hooks at the ends?

Lobster Trap and Fish Tail, mobile, Alexander Calder, collection of the Museum of Modern Art, New York, gift of the Advisory Committee.

Mobile, related shapes balanced and joined with thread.

E. Dyes, enamels and tiles

Three fascinating areas of visual expression that have special appeal to children at this age level are: (1) Designing on cloth by dyeing, (2) Enameling on copper, and (3) Designing mosaics. The interesting thing about each of these art forms is the relative simplicity of the techniques and the high degree of success that a child can achieve as he develops an understanding of the materials being used.

Emphasis should be on color and shape relationships rather than designs containing intricate detail. This should apply to figurative and nonfigurative design alike. While space here will not allow a full description of each process, a few basic suggestions follow. Consult the bibliography for books that focus specifically on each art form.

Designing on cloth by dyeing (batik)

An ancient process, popularized by Indonesian craftsmen, batik is essentially the combination of wax with dyes to create a design on cloth. The design is drawn with wax on the cloth which is then immersed in dye; waxed areas resist the dye and thus form the design. The procedure generally requires a series of wax applications and dye baths, using a variety of colors.

A simplified batik technique is the combination of

wax crayons with a single dye bath, resulting in a multi-color design.

Tools and materials:
Wax crayons, household dye, plain cloth (old pillow cases, sheets), muffin tins, hot plate, electric iron, stiff bristle brushes, a stack of old newspapers.

Activity:
Remove the paper wrappers from the crayons. Break the crayons into small pieces and place in a muffin tin, one color to each section. Place the muffin tin in a pan of water and heat on a hot plate. When the crayons have melted they may be applied to the cloth with brushes. Upon the completion of the design, roll the cloth tightly into a ball. This will crackle the wax crayon colors and add interest to the design. Open the cloth, immerse in dye and hang to dry. The final step is to place the cloth flat between sheets of newspaper and apply a warm iron. This should be repeated until the wax has been removed.

Enameling on copper
The process of enameling on copper has been developed to a highly sophisticated and quite complex art technique by many of today's craftsmen. Projects range from various kinds of jewelry to huge enameled panels forming murals on the facades of today's buildings.

However, for enameling experiences at this age level, the activity should be kept relatively simple. The process is basically the fusing of colored glass in the form of powder, lumps, threads to metal (copper) at a temperature of approximately 1450 degrees.

Tools and materials:
Copper shapes (round, square, rectangle), vials of enamels (powder, lumps, threads), cleaner (Formula 7001), brushes, enameling kiln, firing rack, fork, asbestos gloves.

Activity:
Demonstrate the enameling technique. Prior to the

Batik, wax crayons and single dye bath.

demonstration, all materials should be organized for each step. Heat the kiln to approximately 1450 degrees. Coat the back of the enamel shape with a solution of salt water to prevent or minimize burning. Apply a coat of Formula 7001 to the surface to be enameled. Dust a layer of powdered enamel to the thickness of a thin dime over this. Put the copper shape on the firing rack and, using the fork, place in the heated kiln. Wear asbestos glove during this step. The firing will require one to two minutes. Open the door of the kiln slightly to observe. If the enameled surface is shiny, remove from the kiln and allow to cool.

From this point on, the experience should be one in which the children experiment with different methods of applying enamels to copper shapes to create a design. Completed pieces may be filed (edges) and buffed (reverse side). How can these enameled shapes be used? Pendants? Pins? Cuff links? Findings (pinbacks, etc.) for many different kinds of jewelry may be soldered or glued with epoxy to the reverse sides of enameled shapes.

Designing mosaics

Mosaics are formed by organizing small tiles into a design. The kind of tiles used is a major contributing factor to the ultimate appearance of the mosaic. For example, ceramic tiles may be purchased in a range of brilliant colors. In contrast, a mosaic made of pebbles would be low key in color, relying on subtle variations of tone for the effect.

Tools and materials:

Ceramic tiles, plastic or glass tiles, pebbles, stones, white glue, grout, panels on which to make the mosaic design (plywood, pressed boards), tile cutters.

Activity:

Discuss the characteristics of the mosaic. Emphasize shape, color, textural qualities rather than intricate detail in the design. How can a mosaic be used? Wall panels? Tabletops? Murals? Would a mosaic design be appropriate on a three-dimensional form?

Talk about the different effects that will result from various combinations of materials. Encourage experimentation and handling of the materials as the children plan their design. After the designs have been determined they should be drawn full scale and traced on the board to be used for the mosaic. Then the fun and excitement begin! After all of the tiles have been glued in place it may be desired to add grout to fill in the spaces between tiles. Mix the grout to a creamy consistency, pour on the surface of the mosaic and spread across the tiles with a cardboard squeegee. Allow this to set, then clean the surface with a damp cloth.

F. The poster

Tools and materials:

Colored paper, tempera paints, brushes, tagboard, poster board, paste, glue, scissors, cutting knives.

Emphases:

Understanding the purposes of the poster (to announce an event, promote a service, sell a product).

Understanding the characteristics of the poster.

Applying design concepts to the poster.

Developing skills in lettering and poster illustration.

Activity:

Prepare a bulletin board with examples of posters and related designs. Many booklets, folders and magazine ads have poster-like qualities. Discuss the purposes of the poster. Where are they seen? What do they tell us? How does the poster speak to us: quickly, boldly and in a direct and convincing way? Emphasize the importance of getting the message across quickly since most posters will have an audience that is on the move. Add to this the need for attracting attention.

Talk about the role of the poster in the school and the community. Possible topics may include health, safety, school events, community and world concerns.

In many respects the poster is very closely related to many previous experiences that the children have had — drawing, painting, various techniques of lettering. Printmaking processes such as linoleum, woodcuts and silk screen may be adapted to the poster.

Suggest the making of small preliminary sketches showing possible arrangements of lettering with illustration. From these sketches the child should select one to be enlarged full scale and completed into the final poster. Talk about possible techniques for making the full-size poster. Could an attractive poster be made with the cut and torn paper techniques alone? Try combining cut paper and tempera paint. Some children may wish to use a printmaking process for the illustration and cut paper letters for the slogan. What other materials may be used: scraps, cloth, buttons, yarn, pipe cleaners? Emphasize again that a successful poster gets its message across in a quick, attractive and unusual way.

G. Images and projected images

Rapidly making the scene in elementary as well as secondary school art programs are activities involving the child in the projected image as a means for expanding his concepts of design and communications. Equipment for the projected image would include the slide projector, overhead projector and motion picture projector. The activities suggested here are limited to designing directly on film, acetate or glass, and require little other equipment than that which is normally available in an elementary school. The emphasis should be on the creating of design with light, in combination with a variety of light-altering materials.

Filmmaking by working directly on film

Tools and materials:

16 mm clear leader film, 16 mm opaque (black leader) film, felt pens (various colors), colored inks, dyes, knives, needles, pen points and holders, splicer and splicing tape.

Activity:

Clarify the technicalities related to the film: 16 frames per second on silent speed, 24 frames on sound speed. Frames pass through the projector horizontally. To create the illusion of movement, change or increase the size of a shape or object. Allow five to six frames for each step. For example, a face would go through several steps in a change from a smile to a frown. Each step should be repeated on five or six frames of film. This will allow the eye to perceive the transition when the film is projected.

An initial activity with clear leader film should allow the children to experiment with felt pens and colored inks, or with pointed instruments to scratch designs into opaque leader film. Thirty feet of film will project about fifty seconds. Several children may work together on one length of film or it may be cut into shorter lengths and spliced together after individual designs are completed.

Slides and acetate

Almost any material that will effect the passage or blockage of light produced by an overhead or slide projector may be used: colored tissue, colored inks, lacquer paints, felt pens, crayons, paper or cardboard shapes, natural objects. Wet colors may be intermingled on a sheet of glass or acetate positioned on an overhead projector. This will produce fascinating, ever-changing designs right before the eyes of the audience. The addition of music will bring more excitement to the creative environment.

Two by two inch glass slides will fit most projectors. Designs may be developed directly on a single glass slide or by using light-altering materials sandwiched in between two such slides.

H. Pulling strings

Throughout the elementary school experience, children have engaged in numerous puppet activities: stick, bag, sock and variations. Marionettes or string puppets require considerably more skill in construction and operation than hand puppets and are more appropriate for this age level. Figures, animals, fantasy and imagination are just as much a part of the activity at this time as before. Stories, songs and original scripts by the children may serve as motivation for the activity.

Technically, it should be emphasized that all of the

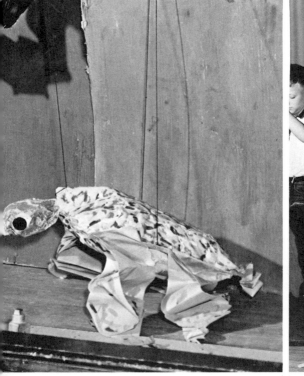

joints of a string puppet should be flexible so that the legs, arms, and head may move. This is vital to a successful performance.

The body of the puppet may be made out of wood parts or a stuffed cloth form.

Wood:

The torso or body should be made out of a block of soft wood. Wood dowels are cut for the lower legs, upper legs, lower arms and upper arms. Hands and feet may be carved from wood or made out of papier pulp mache. These parts are joined with screw eyes or cloth tape so that they will have free movement. The head may be formed out of mache and attached to the top of the body with tape or screw eyes.

Cloth:

Draw the entire figure on a double layer of cloth. Cut out and sew together each part: lower legs, upper legs, torso, etc. Leave necessary opening in each part to allow turning the seam inward and for stuffing. Stuff the parts, insert weights in bottom of torso and at lower end of limbs, sew up openings and join the parts. Head, hands and feet may be made as described under "wood" and attached.

Costumes should be loose enough to allow free movement of all parts.

String puppet controls:

Three wood strips approximately one inch wide, six to seven inches long, one-quarter of an inch thick, are required for the controls of the puppet. Nail one strip across and about two inches from the end of a second strip. Drive a nail into but not through the other end of the second strip. Bore a hole in the middle of the third strip so it can fit over the nail. The controls now consist of two parts: (1) The fixed crosspiece (main control) holds the puppet, (2) The removable stick "walks" the puppet.

The strings:

After the puppet is completed and costumed, attach the control strings (strong nylon thread). Bore holes in the control sticks as follows: one at each end of the fixed crosspiece for head control, one at each end of removable crosspiece for control of feet, one at front end of main control stick for hands, one at the middle of main control stick for control of shoulders, one at back of main control stick for control of hip section of puppet. After determining the desired length of the control strings, attach them, running each from its appropriate part to related holes in the control stick.

CREATING AN ENVIRONMENT FOR VISUAL EXPRESSION

Planning and organizing are two words that are familiar to the classroom teacher. Perhaps in educational terminology that is what this entire section is about. However, it is hoped that the real focus will be on the spirit that may be produced through a well thought out program of art experiences at each age level.

1. A room environment that challenges the imagination of the child and encourages a creative response

Is the classroom (physical space) one in which the children are interested, excited? Are there bright, lively colors, captivating pictures? Are there things to talk about — curious things, fascinating things — on display? A table full of objects that can be picked up

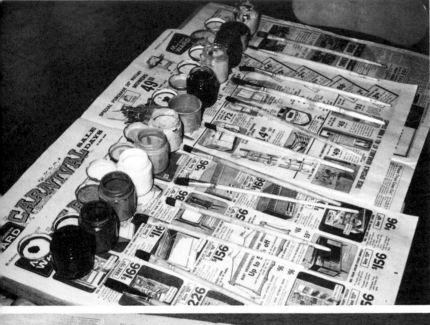

by the children, handled, discussed and used in art activities, should be located in a prominent part of the room. Shells, pebbles, boxes of assorted sizes, found objects, yarn, scrap wood, and countless other items that will arouse curiosity, stimulate thinking and help develop understanding of color, texture, shape, form, should be included.

Are the bulletin boards dynamic, attention-getting, frequently changed? Bulletin boards are tremendous teaching devices. Try using them, (1) as a focal point for presenting a lesson, (2) as a means for clarifying an art process or an art film, (3) to display the children's art work. Can you set aside one part of the bulletin board for the SCHOOL ARTISTS OF THE WEEK? Construct a progressive bulletin board. For example, when cardboard printing is planned in the program, three or four days prior to introducing the activity, arrange a few imaginative cardboard shapes on one part of the bulletin board. Say nothing. The next day add three or four cardboard prints and the cardboard plate used to make the prints. This should be followed by adding the title and captions. The reaction of the children will be surprising.

Are the tools and materials for the art program readily available to the children? For smooth operation, tools and materials should be organized according to specific art activities. Quantity, of course, is based on the number of children participating. Some general suggestions follow:

Tempera painting

Liquid tempera — pint jars, at least one of each color and two of white and black. Transfer approximately one inch of each color to small jars, with lids, to provide a set for one to four children.

Powdered tempera — pound cans.

Drawing paper — newsprint, 12" x 18" or 18" x 24"; white drawing paper, 12" x 18", or 18" x 24".

Brushes — 1/2" and 3/4" flat bristle; provide one brush for each color or thoroughly instruct the child in cleaning the brush when changing colors.

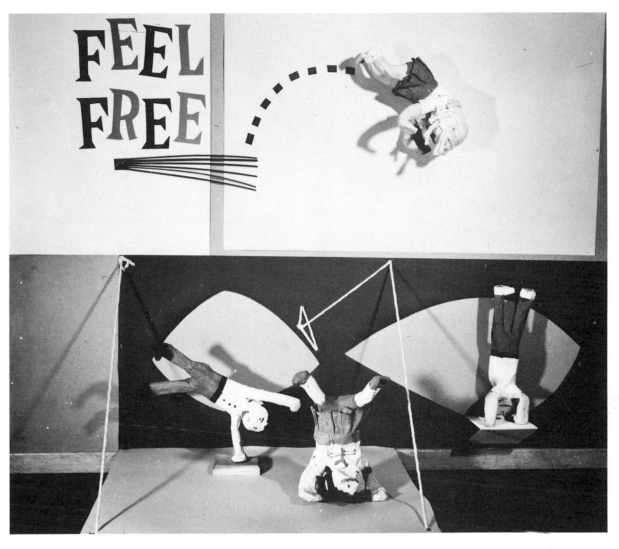

Containers for mixing colors, containers for clear water (large jars or coffee cans), tongue depressors for stirring paints, aprons or smocks for each child; newspapers, paper towels, rags, sponge and bucket of water.

Finger painting

Finger paint colors — range of colors for group of four to six children; tongue depressor for each color.

Finger paint paper — 12'' x 16'' or 16'' x 22''; several sheets available for each child.

Flat pan of water to soak paper, oilcloth large enough to cover work spaces, paper towels, aprons or smocks, newspapers, sponge and bucket of water for clean-up.

Mural painting

Brown Kraft Paper, 36'' wide; one roll will last over an extended period of time. **Project paper**, 36'' wide, rolls; variety of colors. Chalks, tempera paints, colored construction paper, 9'' x 12'' or 12'' x 18'', usually 100 sheets (solid or assorted colors) to a package.

Drawing with chalks

Assorted colors, one box for each child; 12'' x 18'', 18'' x 24'' white drawing paper, bogus, manila (usually 500 sheets to a package); colored construction paper 18'' x 24''.

Drawing with crayons

Assorted colors, wax, eight colors to a box, one box for each child. Crayon refills packaged single color to a box. White drawing paper, 12'' x 18'' or 18'' x 24'', 500 sheets to a package.

Lettering

There is a wide variety of felt pens, Speedball and other brands of pens, steel brushes, and ox and camel hair brushes available for making many different styles and sizes of letter forms. As the student becomes familiar with these tools and acquires some control over their use, he will find many applications for lettering. Captions, titles and slogans for bulletin boards, charts, folders, science projects, posters, and program covers are a few of the items which lend themselves to individual expression in lettering.

Printmaking

Many of the simpler techniques require only standard materials. For example, for scrap and cardboard printing, use cardboard, tubing, or found objects; print with tempera paint. For linoleum block printing, use linoleum mounted on wood blocks, or unmounted linoleum, cutting tools with interchangeable blades (v-shaped veiners and u-shaped gouges). To hold linoleum firmly in place while cutting the design, use a block stop of wood, size 7½" x 11¼." A block stop for each child is recommended. In a class-wide activity, organize four to six inking stations. Each station should have a 12" x 12" inking slab (plate glass, vinyl tile, or sheet metal), a rubber brayer, one tube of water-base ink, and a jar of water to add to the ink if it dries out.

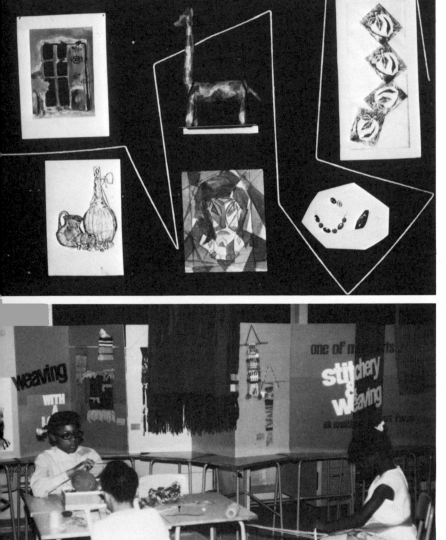

Ceramic clay

Moist white clay comes ready for use in 50-pound containers. One container or drum of 50 pounds should be sufficient for a beginning class in clay activities. It is recommended that cone 06 clay, which fires to approximately 1830 degrees Fahrenheit, be used. When not being used, clay should be kept in air-tight containers to prevent drying. Work in progress should be enclosed in plastic bags. Many different overglazes and underglazes are available in both powder and liquid form, and in a wide variety of colors. Overglazes fire to a shiny, matte, or crackled finish, depending upon the type used. Underglazes fire to a relatively soft finish, and often a clear glaze is applied over the underglaze to produce a hard, durable finish. Underglaze may be applied to greenware (unfired objects) before firing. Overglaze should, generally, be used on pieces that have been bisque fired — the process of firing at a temperature considerably below the maturing temperature of the overglaze. The maturing temperature of overglaze should match that of the clay. For example, cone 06 glazes should be used with cone 06 clay.

Textiles

Gingham, muslins, burlap (available in a variety of colors) and monk's cloth, are good cloth materials for stitchery projects. Other items for this activity would include pearl cotton thread, colored twine, yarns, and needles with blunt points and big eyes. Stitchery kits are available through art materials suppliers. One kit usually contains all that is needed for the average class.

Weaving materials are generally determined by the process. Cardboard, box, or frame looms require warp which may be purchased by the spool, tube or skein. Other materials, including string, grasses, raffia, plastics may be used for weaving.

Papier-Mâché (Masks, figures, animals)

The basic material to be purchased is wheat paste. This is a floury material that is mixed with water to a creamy consistency for papier-mâché work. A five pound package of this paperhanger's paste goes a long way.

Other materials

Newsprint and manila paper, 18" x 24", 500 sheets to a package. Paints, chalks and crayons work well on these papers. Tag board, 9" x 12", 12" x 18" and 18" x 24", for painting, posters, construction.

Bristol board, 22" x 28" (white); **poster board,** 22" x 28" (assorted colors); **Mat board,** 22" x 28" (white one side, pebbled surface) for painting, posters, construction. Mat board is popular for mounting or matting the children's paintings, drawings, and for prints. These materials may be purchased in single sheets.

Colored tissue, many brilliant colors; various sizes, 15" x 20", 20" x 30", from 25 to 500 sheets (solid colors or assorted colors) per package; for collage, cut and torn paper work, backgrounds for printmaking.

Crayons, box of eight assorted colors, wax; various sizes, 5/16" x 3-1/2", 1/2" x 4" (larger size recommended for younger children). Refills are usually packaged one dozen of one color per box.

Chalks, large size 1" x 4", 12 assorted colors to a box; a group of four children may share one box.

Scissors, 5", lightweight, pointed; one pair for each child.

Stencil knives, with replacement blades for cutting cardboard, carving plaster, and wood.

Adhesives: white glue, 4 oz. squeeze bottle; rubber cement, 4 oz. bottle, half pint can, pint can with brush; library paste, quart jars.

Staple gun and staples for bulletin board work; desk stapler for paper sculpture, mounting pictures, and various other paper activities; one of each per teacher.

Interesting materials to collect and use

For making masks and puppets: paper bags, cloth remnants, socks, ribbons, buttons, costume jewelry.

For making mobiles, stabiles, figures: scraps of soft metal, wire, coat hangers, miscellaneous items for decorating.

For making mosaics: colored glass bottles that may be broken in pieces, scrap tile in various colors, pebbles of various sizes.

For collage, assemblages, rubbings, printmaking, constructions, texturing: boxes, cartons, trays, nails, saw blades, scrap wood, combs, spools, beads, colored cellophane, cardboard tubing, corrugated cardboard, sandpaper, found objects, sticks, weeds and grasses, small branches, leaves, tree bark, pebbles, bottle stoppers and tops, and other items children can bring from home, community, nature.

For simple loom weaving and silk screening: picture frames, boxes, box lids, cardboard, embroidery hoops.

When shelving and storeroom facilities are limited, materials and tools may be organized and stored in cardboard cartons, painted bright colors and labeled according to art activity. Children's flatwork (drawings, paintings, textiles) may be stored in portfolios. Shelving for three-dimensional objects may be made by laying 1'' x 10'' x 6' wood planks on cinder blocks. These materials provide opportunity for making several shelves, requiring a minimum of wall space.

A good substitute for built-in bulletin boards is the side of a corrugated mattress carton. This can be trimmed, painted and positioned on the ledge of a chalkboard. A 4' x 8' sheet of soft wallboard is also very effective as a bulletin board.

2. A program that challenges the imagination of the child, encourages a creative response and provides time for meaningful visual expression.

A specific time should be allotted in the weekly school program for art appreciation, environmental awareness and creative art activities. This may vary from 100 to 150 minutes. A major guideline, however, should be the child's interest in what he is doing. Too often a child's involvement in art has reached a high level and because of rigid scheduling he has to stop and pursue some other activity. Thus, it is recommended that the special time for art should be established with some flexibility. Additional time on other days may be considered to meet special interests or to just listen and watch the child as he explores ideas. Then too, the art process can become a part of other aspects of the curriculum — science displays, maps, school events, social studies murals and dioramas.

The program of art at each age level should be based upon the interests and capabilities of the children. At times this would be in the direction of individual art projects, other times, group activities. In preparing for the art experience consider: (1) Interests and capabilities of the child, (2) A balanced two- and three-dimensional art program, (3) Provision for the children to work independently to search, to discover and to develop their own ideas, (4) Skills, techniques and processes learned previously, (5) The motivational value of films, film-strips, music, prints, demonstration, field trips, (6) The feasibility of and potential for working outside of the classroom: sketching, painting, sand casting, sculpturing.

The key role of the teacher while the children are engaged in creative art activities should be to OBSERVE, ENCOURAGE and to move around the room giving individual assistance, answering questions as the need arises. At times it may be useful to re-demonstrate a technique, process or use of a material for the entire class. Provide the children with simple, direct and relevant answers to their questions. They know when they need help and vague replies or innocuous comments will not satisfy them.

Evaluation should be an on-going process. Younger children continually and quite naturally critique their own work. This should be encouraged. More formal evaluation should be, (1) conducted on an individual basis, helping the child to SEE his art work in relation to understandings being developed (design concepts, skills, etc.), (2) organized to allow children time to evaluate each other's work. Emphasize successes.

3. Additional notes on materials.

Mosaics and commercial ceramic tiles

Ceramic tiles may be purchased in 12″ x 12″ sheets and a wide variety of colors. Individual tiles are approximately 13/16″ square. Sheets of tiles should be soaked in clear water, tiles removed and stored in containers according to color. Ceramic tiles may be cut into smaller sizes and different shapes with end-cutting nippers. Tile cement or white glue may be used to fix tiles to a surface. Grout, a white waterproof cement, may be used to fill in the space between tiles in a mosaic. Mixed to a creamy consistency, the grout is poured over the mosaic design and spread with a rubber squeegee (or cardboard shape). Excess grout should be wiped off with a damp sponge or cloth and the design allowed to dry. Colored glass tiles may be used in the same way.

Carving materials.

Simulated stone: A simulated stone may be made from cement, plaster of Paris, sand and vermiculite. Various combinations, thoroughly mixed before adding water, produce different kinds of basic materials for carving. Mixture 1: one part sand, one part cement, three parts vermiculite. Mixture 2: one part sand, one part cement, one part plaster of Paris, four parts vermiculite. Mixture 3: two parts plaster of Paris, one part sand, three parts vermiculite. Dry or liquid tempera may be added for color. After adding water, the various mixtures may be poured into cardboard cartons to solidify.

Plaster of Paris: Fill a plastic pan with an amount

of water equal to the desired amount of plaster. Sift the plaster into the water until it begins to build a peak above the water. Mix carefully to avoid bubbles. As soon as the plaster begins to thicken, pour it into cardboard containers. Liquid tempera and vegetable colors may be added to provide coloring. Variations: Sawdust may be added to the plaster to produce texture. One part baking soda to twenty parts of plaster will cause the plaster to bubble, creating a porous and softer carving material.

Painting

Water base paints may be changed to adhere to waxy or oily surfaces by adding detergent. A spatter effect may be achieved in painting by dipping a toothbrush in tempera paint and scrubbing it across a piece of mesh or screening held several inches above the painting surface.

A little oil of cloves or wintergreen may be added to tempera paint to prevent souring.

Finger painting

One-half cup of starch dissolved in water and added to one quart of hot water, plus liquid or powdered tempera for color, will make a good finger paint with a pasty consistency.

Flour paste

One-half cup of sifted flour with two cups of cold water added slowly, will make a smooth paste.

Papier-mâché paste

One cup of flour, two cups of boiling water, two teaspoons of liquid glue and a few drops of oil of cloves will make a creamy paste.

Library paste

Mix two tablespoons of minute tapioca, three tablespoons of sugar, one teaspoon of vinegar, one pinch of salt and one cup of boiling water and cook in a double boiler until thick. The resultant paste is ready for use as soon as it is cool.

Silk-screen paint, water base

Mix equal parts of powdered tempera and liquid starch plus enough water to make a "pudding" consistency.

Modeling materials

Paper pulp: Tear newspaper into small bits. Soak well in water. Drain water and add wheat paste to the consistency of soft modeling clay. Add a few drops of oil of cloves or wintergreen to serve as a preservative.

Papier-mâché, strip method: Tear newspaper into long, narrow strips. Dip strips into wheat paste and cover prepared form, criss-crossing strips, until desired thickness is achieved.

Papier-mâché, sheet method: Smooth a layer of wheat paste over a sheet of newspaper. Place another sheet of newspaper over this. Cover the second sheet with wheat paste and repeat the process until six or eight layers have been applied. When this has become leathery in quality, it may be cut, molded and shaped into a desired form.

Plaster of Paris. Mix two parts plaster of Paris, one part wheat paste and four parts sawdust. Add one to two cups of water. This will make a smooth mixture for modeling puppet heads.

Sawdust, woodshavings: (1) Wheat paste may be added to sawdust to produce a modeling material. (2) Liquid glue may be added to sawdust to form a thick paste which when dry may be sawed, filed, whittled, or sanded. (3) Wood shavings mixed with wheat paste makes a modeling material that is suitable for mask-making. Completed masks may be decorated with paint.

Glossary

ABSTRACT ART — A style in which the artist selects or abstracts parts of figures, scenes or objects and reassembles them in a new way to accentuate a point of view that the eye would not normally see without representation or realistic elements.

ABSTRACT EXPRESSIONISM — A style of painting in which images and colors are painted on the canvas in a random and spontaneous way.

ASSEMBLAGE — A sculptural technique of organizing into a unified product, a group of unrelated, fragmented or discarded objects.

BALANCE — The arrangement of the visual elements in a design. It may be formal or symmetrical (both sides of the design the same); informal or asymmetrical (contrasting elements in the design), or radial (design elements radiating from a central axis).

BASIC STITCHES — Running, chain, couching, satin, outline, blanket, cross, feather.

BATIK — Combination of wax and dye to create a design on fabric. A technique.

BISQUE WARE — Clay product after first firing.

BRAYER — Rubber composition roller used to prepare and to apply ink to a block or plate; also used to apply ink directly to a surface in developing a design.

CALLIGRAPHY — Beautiful lettering. In painting, lines and shapes that are derived from or resemble letter forms and are characterized by qualities usually associated with Chinese brush lettering.

CARVING — A subtractive sculptural technique; cutting away from a block or solid mass.

CERAMICS — Process of producing or forming objects out of wet clay by firing at high temperatures.

COLLAGE — Art form introduced by Cubists and developed further by Dadaists. Originally, the cutting and pasting of a variety of papers to form design.

COMMERCIAL ART — Graphic design; art used to project the image of industry and products.

CONSTRUCTING — Fabricating a sculptural form using various three-dimensional materials such as wire, wood, metal, found objects.

CUBISM — A style of painting and sculpture developed in the early 20th century, characterized by the simplification of natural forms to their geometrical equivalents.

DRAWING MATERIALS — Pencils, crayons, pens, inks, chalks, charcoal.

ENAMELING — Fusing of powdered glass (enamels) to metal, principally copper.

ENAMELS — Powdered glass of various colors; also in the form of lumps and threads.

ENVIRONMENT — Man's dwelling place in every respect: housing, transportation, signs, lighting, natural and man-made forms.

EXPRESSIONISM — An art style of the early 20th century in which objects are purposely distorted and colors changed or intensified to reflect inner emotion rather than actual appearance.

FORM — Visual aspects or shape of a work of art.

FOUND OBJECTS — Discarded utensils, containers, parts of machinery, manufactured for purposes other than the uses made of them by children and artists.

FREE FORM — Non-realistic shapes made by an artist for a specific purpose.

FUTURISM — A 20th century style of painting that attempts to show movement by multiple image repetition of shapes.

GREENWARE — Clay product before firing; leather hard.

HUE — A color.

IMPRESSIONISM — A late 19th century movement in painting, concerned with the development of unusual techniques for applying color to express qualities of atmosphere and light.

INTENSITY — Brightness or dullness of a color.

KILN — Furnace, heated by gas, wood, or electricity, for firing ceramic ware.

KINETIC SCULPTURE — A sculpture form designed to move by touch, electricity or other means.

LETTERING — Styles: capitals, lower case, roman, italic, bold, light, condensed, standard, extended.

LOOM — A frame or machine for interweaving yarn or thread into fabric.

MASS — Solid physical weight in a sculptured form.

MEDIUM — A specific material or element such as clay for pottery, oil paints for painting.

MOBILE SCULPTURE — A sculpture, usually suspended, in which parts move in a rhythmical synthesis of form, balance and motion.

MODELING — An additive sculptural technique; building a form with a plastic material such as clay.

MONOPRINT — A printmaking technique that generally results in a single print.

MOSAIC — A design comprised of small tiles of stone, ceramic, glass, wood.

MURAL — A wall painting. Children's murals are made to fit a wall space but not actually painted on the wall.

NEGATIVE SPACE — Empty spaces between important images in a painting. The negative space contributes to the unity of the whole painting.

NON-OBJECTIVE ART — Also called non-representational art because the forms or shapes are not intended to look like real objects. Both painting and sculpture can be non-objective.

OP ART — A contemporary painting style in which the juxtaposition of colors and lines causes the viewer to see optical illusions. Things in the picture appear to move or jump.

PAPIER-MÂCHÉ — Paper pulp or torn paper strips covered with paste or other binder and used over an armature to model figures, animals, masks.

POP ART — A contemporary style which tends to glorify ordinary objects of trade: soup cans, coke bottles, shoes and the like.

PRIMITIVE ART — The work of a naïve or untaught artist. The art of a preliterate civilization. Examples: The Maya of Mexico, The Inca of Peru.

PRINTMAKING — Duplicating a design by transferring it from a prepared surface to another surface.

REALISM — A movement in painting and sculpture which advocates true to life appearance.

RELIEF PRINT — Print made from raised surfaces on a block: linoleum, wood, plaster, etc.

REPRESENTATIONAL — Figurative, identifiable subject matter.

SCULPTURE — Design utilizing materials in three-dimensional form.

STENCIL — A block-out printing technique. Stencils may be used alone or in connection with a silk screen.

STITCHERY — The application of design to fabric by using various stitches, threads and other materials; includes stitching of shapes of cloth to fabric (appliqué).

SURFACE DECORATION (CLAY) — Design added to surface of greenware by carving, incising, underglazing, etc., or to bisque ware by glazing.

SURREALISM — A 20th century art style stressing the subconscious or non-rational significance of images. The paintings have a dreamlike, frequently uneasy quality.

TEMPERA — A painting medium characterized by its non-transparent, opaque effect.

TESSERAE — Tiles used in making mosaics.

TEXTILES — Woven fabrics.

TEXTURE — A visual element that identifies surface quality in a real or implied sense as being rough, smooth, soft.

THREE-DIMENSIONAL FORM — Sculpture, architecture and construction.

TIE-DYEING — A process of hand dyeing fabric, a portion of which is tightly bound with thread to resist the dye solution.

TRANSPARENT WATERCOLOR — A transparent painting medium.

VALUE — Lightness or darkness of a color.

WARP — Threads arranged lengthwise on a loom.

WEFT — Threads woven across warp threads on a loom.

Books

GENERAL

THE PROCESS OF ART EDUCATION IN THE ELEMENTARY SCHOOL — George Conrad: Prentice-Hall, Englewood Cliffs, N.J. 1964.

TEACHING ART TO CHILDREN — Blanche Jefferson: Allyn and Bacon, Inc., Boston, 1959.

DO YOU SEE WHAT I SEE?— Helen Borten: Abelard-Schuman, New York, 1959.

ART MEDIA FOR YOUNG PEOPLE — Pearl Greenberg: Van Nostrand Reinhold, New York, 1970.

ART FOR CITY CHILDREN — Norman Krinsky: Van Nostrand Reinhold, New York, 1970.

LEARNING TO SEE — Kurt Rowland: Van Nostrand Reinhold, New York, 1970.

CREATING PAINTING WITH TEMPERA — Pauline Albenda: Van Nostrand Reinhold, New York, 1970.

TEACHING COLOR AND FORM — Gottfried Tritten: Van Nostrand Reinhold, New York, 1970.

BULLETIN BOARDS — George F. Horn: Van Nostrand Reinhold, New York, 1962.

GROWING WITH CHILDREN THROUGH ART — Aida Cannarsa Snow: Van Nostrand Reinhold, New York, 1968.

WITH A FREE HAND — Adelaide Sproul: Van Nostrand Reinhold, New York, 1968.

WAYS WITH ART — Harold Stevens: Van Nostrand Reinhold, New York, 1963.

PAINTING FOR CHILDREN — Lois T. Horne: Van Nostrand Reinhold, New York, 1968.

REINHOLD VISUALS — John Lidstone, Stanley T. Lewis, and Sheldon Brody: Van Nostrand Reinhold, New York, 1968. Portfolio 1—Line, Portfolio 2—Mass, Portfolio 3—Organization, Portfolio 4—Surface, Portfolio 5—Color, Portfolio 6—Movement, Portfolio 7—Perception, Portfolio 8—Space, 1969.

SELF EXPRESSION IN CLASSROOM ART — Material . . . Process . . . Idea — John Lidstone: Davis Publications, Inc., Worcester, Mass., 1967.

BULLETIN BOARDS AND DISPLAY — Reino Randall and Edward C. Haines: Davis Publications, Inc., Worcester, Mass., 1963.

DESIGN ACTIVITIES FOR THE ELEMENTARY CLASSROOM — John Lidstone: Davis Publications, Inc., Worcester, Mass., 1964.

HOW TO PREPARE VISUAL MATERIALS FOR SCHOOL USE — George F. Horn: Davis Publications, Inc., Worcester, Mass., 1963.

CREATIVE AND MENTAL GROWTH — Viktor Lowenfeld and W. Lambert Brittain: MacMillan Co., New York, 1964.

DEVELOPING ARTISTIC AND PERCEPTUAL AWARENESS — Earl W. Linderman and Donald W. Heberholz: Wm. C. Brown Co., Dubuque, Iowa, 1964.

EDUCATION THROUGH ART — Sir Herbert Read: Pantheon Books, New York, 1958.

ART ACTIVITIES FOR THE VERY YOUNG — F. Louis Hoover: Davis Publications, Inc., Worcester, Mass., 1961.

DESIGN

DESIGN IN NATURE — Vivian Varney Guyler: Davis Publications, Inc., Worcester, Mass., 1970.

DESIGNING WITH LIGHT, on Paper and Film — Robert W. Cooke: Davis Publications, Inc., Worcester, Mass., 1969.

DESIGN IN THREE DIMENSIONS — Reino Randall and Edward C. Haines: Davis Publications, Inc., Worcester, Mass., 1965.

DRAWING AND PAINTING

THE CRAYON — George F. Horn: Davis Publications, Inc., Worcester, Mass., 1969.

PAINTING IN THE SCHOOL PROGRAM — Virginia G. Timmons: Davis Publications, Inc., Worcester, Mass., 1968.

EXPLORING PAINT — Henry Petterson and Ray Gerring: Van Nostrand Reinhold, New York, 1964.

SKETCHING WITH THE FELT-TIP PEN — Henry C. Pitz: Studio Publications, Inc., New York, 1959.

CHILDREN'S EXPERIENCES IN ART — Pearl Greenberg: Van Nostrand Reinhold, New York, 1966.

TECHNIQUES OF PICTURE MAKING — Henry M. Gasser: Van Nostrand Reinhold, New York, 1962.

ART TECHNIQUES FOR CHILDREN — Gottfried Tritten: Van Nostrand Reinhold, New York, 1964.

LET'S MAKE A MURAL — Marjorie Kelly and Nicholas Roukes: Fearon Publishers, San Francisco, 1959.

EXPLORING FINGER PAINT — Victoria Betts: Davis Publications, Inc., Worcester, Mass., 1963.

MURALS FOR SCHOOLS — Arne W. Randall: Davis Publications, Inc., Worcester, Mass., 1961.

CREATIVE DRAWING, Point and Line — Ernst Rottger and Dieter Klante: Van Nostrand Reinhold, New York, 1963.

CREATIVE EXPRESSION WITH CRAYONS — E. Reid Boylston: Davis Publications, Inc., Worcester, Mass., 1954.

PRINTMAKING

GRAPHIC DESIGN — Mathew Baranski: International Textbook Co., Scranton, Penn., 1960.

SILK SCREEN AS A FINE ART — Clifford Chieffo: Van Nostrand Reinhold, New York, 1967.

PRINTMAKING WITHOUT A PRESS — Jane D. Erickson and Adelaide Sproul: Van Nostrand Reinhold, New York, 1966.

PRINTS AND HOW TO MAKE THEM — Arthur Zaidenberg: Harper and Row, New York, 1964.

YOUNG PRINTMAKERS, II, Portfolio — Edited by F. Louis Hoover: Davis Publications, Inc., Worcester, Mass., 1969.

SERIGRAPHY: SILK SCREEN TECHNIQUES FOR THE ARTIST — Auvil: Van Nostrand Reinhold, New York, 1966.

PRINTMAKING WITH A SPOON — Norman Gorbaty: Van Nostrand Reinhold, New York, 1960.

PRINTMAKING TODAY — Jules Heller: Holt, Rinehart and Winston, Inc., New York, 1958.

NEW CREATIVE PRINT MAKING — Peter Green: Watson-Guptill Publishing Co., New York, 1964.

PRINTMAKING ACTIVITIES FOR THE CLASSROOM — W. Arnel Pattemore: Davis Publications, Inc., Worcester, Mass., 1966.

RELIEF PRINTMAKING — Gerald F. Brommer: Davis Publications, Inc., Worcester, Mass., 1970.

LETTERING, POSTERS, CARTOONING

WORDS AND CALLIGRAPHY FOR CHILDREN — John W. Cataldo: Van Nostrand Reinhold, New York, 1969.

LETTERING ART IN MODERN USE — Raymond A. Ballinger: Van Nostrand Reinhold, New York, 1965.

LETTERING: A GUIDE FOR TEACHERS — John W. Cataldo: Davis Publications, Inc., Worcester, Mass., 1966.

LETTERING: Charles R. Anderson: Van Nostrand Reinhold, New York, 1969.

POSTERS: DESIGNING, MAKING, REPRO-
DUCING — George F. Horn: Davis Publications, Inc., Worcester, Mass., 1964.

CARTOONING — George F. Horn: Davis Publications, Inc., Worcester, Mass., 1965.

SCULPTURE

SAND SCULPTURING — Mickey Klar Marks:
Dial Press, New York, 1962.

CERAMIC SCULPTURE — Betty Davenport
Ford: Van Nostrand Reinhold, New York,
1964.

TOY SCULPTURE — William Accorsi: Van
Nostrand Reinhold, New York, 1968.

SCULPTURE FROM JUNK — Henry Rasmusen
and Art Grant: Van Nostrand Reinhold, New
York, 1967.

HOW TO MAKE SHAPES IN SPACE — Toni
Hughes: E. P. Dutton and Co., New York,
1955.

CREATING WITH PLASTER — Dona Meilach:
Reilly and Lee, Chicago, 1966.

CLAY, WOOD AND WIRE — Harvey Weiss:
William R. Scott, Inc., New York, 1956.

YOUNG SCULPTORS, Portfolio — F. Louis
Hoover: Davis Publications, Inc., Worcester,
Mass., 1967.

CONSTRUCTION: Wood, paper, wire

PLAY WITH PAPER — Thea Bank-Jensen:
Macmillan Co., New York, 1962.

BUILDING WITH BALSA WOOD — John
Lidstone: Van Nostrand Reinhold, New York,
1965.

ART FROM SCRAP — Carl Reed and Joseph
Orze: Davis Publications Inc., Worcester, Mass.,
1962.

WIRE SCULPTURE AND OTHER THREE-
DIMENSIONAL CONSTRUCTION — Gerald F.
Brommer: Davis Publications, Inc., Worcester,
Mass., 1968.

DESIGN IN THREE DIMENSIONS — Reino
Randall and Edward C. Haines: Davis Publications, Inc., Worcester, Mass., 1965.

PAPER SCULPTURE — Mary Grace Johnston:
Davis Publications, Inc., Worcester, Mass.,
1965.

HOW TO MAKE MOBILES — John Lynch:
Viking Press, New York, 1953.

EXPLORING PAPIER-MÂCHÉ — Victoria B.
Betts: Davis Publications, Inc., Worcester,
Mass., 1955.

SCULPTURE IN PAPER — Ralph Fabri: Watson-Guptill Publishing Co., New York, 1966.

CREATING WITH PAPER — Pauline Johnson: University of Washington Press, Seattle, 1958.

CREATIVE PAPER DESIGN — Ernst Rottger: Van Nostrand Reinhold, New York, 1961.

WOODEN IMAGES — Norman Laliberté and Maureen Jones: Van Nostrand Reinhold, New York, 1966.

CREATIVE WOOD DESIGN — Ernst Rottger: Van Nostrand Reinhold, New York, 1961.

COLLAGE AND CONSTRUCTION IN SCHOOL — Preschool/Junior High — Lois Lord: Davis Publications, Inc., Worcester, Mass., 1970.

COLLAGE AND FOUND ART — Dona Meilach and Elvie Ten Hoor: Van Nostrand Reinhold, New York, 1964.

CREATING WITH CORRUGATED PAPER — Rolf Hartung: Van Nostrand Reinhold, New York, 1966.

PAPER CONSTRUCTION FOR CHILDREN — Norman Krinsky and Bill Berry: Van Nostrand Reinhold, New York, 1966.

BUILDING WITH CARDBOARD — John Lidstone: Van Nostrand, Reinhold, New York, 1968.

CREATIVE PAPER DESIGN — Ernst Rottger: Van Nostrand Reinhold, New York, 1961.

CRAFTS:
Ceramics, Mosaics, Textiles, Enameling

CRAFTS DESIGN, An Illustrated Guide — Spencer Mosely, Pauline Johnson and Hazel Koenig: Wadsworth Publishing Co., Belmont, Calif., 1962.

CREATIVE ARTS AND CRAFTS ACTIVITIES — Arthur S. Green: T.S. Denison and Co., Inc., Minneapolis, 1960.

CERAMIC SCULPTURE — Betty Davenport Ford: Van Nostrand Reinhold, New York, 1964.

CERAMIC DESIGN — John B. Kenny: Chilton Book Co., Philadelphia, 1962.

CLAY IN THE CLASSROOM — George Barford: Davis Publications, Inc., Worcester, Mass., 1963.

MAKING POTTERY WITHOUT A WHEEL — F. Carlton Ball and Janice Lovoos: Van Nostrand Reinhold, New York, 1965.

CERAMIC ART IN THE SCHOOL PROGRAM — Thomas G. Supensky: Davis Publications, Inc., Worcester, Mass., 1968.

CREATING FORM IN CLAY — Henry Petterson: Van Nostrand Reinhold, New York, 1968.

POTTERY STEP-BY-STEP — Henry Trevor: Watson-Guptill Publications, Cincinnati, 1966.

THE TECHNIQUE OF HANDBUILT POTTERY — Mollie Winterburn: Watson-Guptill Publications, Cincinnati, 1969.

CREATIVE CLAY DESIGN — Ernst Rottger: Van Nostrand Reinhold, New York, 1963.

MOSAIC MAKING — Helen Hutton: Van Nostrand Reinhold, NewYork, 1966.

MODERN MOSAIC TECHNIQUES — Janice Lovoos and Felice Paramore: Watson-Guptill Publishing Co., New York, 1967.

MOSAIC ART TODAY — Larry Argiro: International Texbook Co., Scranton, Penn., 1961.

BATIK — Nik Krevitsky: Van Nostrand Reinhold, New York, 1964.

STITCHERY, ART AND CRAFT — Nik Krevitsky: Van Nostrand Reinhold, New York, 1966.

APPLIQUÉ STITCHERY — Jean Ray Laury: Van Nostrand Reinhold, New York, 1966.

RAG TAPESTRIES AND WOOL MOSAICS — Ann Wiseman: Van Nostrand Reinhold, New York, 1969.

CREATIVE USE OF STITCHES — Vera P. Guild: Davis Publications, Inc., Worcester, Mass. (Revised 1969).

ADVENTURE IN STITCHES — Karasz: Watson-Guptill Publications, Cincinnati (Revised 1959).

MORE CREATIVE TEXTILE DESIGN — Rolf Hartung: Van Nostrand Reinhold, New York, 1964.

WEAVING WITHOUT A LOOM — Sarita Rainey: Davis Publications, Inc., Worcester, Mass., 1965.

THE TECHNIQUES OF RUG WEAVING —

Peter Collingwood: Watson-Guptill Publications, Cincinnati, 1969.

CREATE WITH YARN — Ethel Jane Beitler: International Textbook Co., Scranton, Penn., 1964.

STITCHERY FOR CHILDREN — Jacqueline Enthoven: Van Nostrand Reinhold, New York, 1968.

THE COMPLETE BOOK OF RUG HOOKING — Barbara J. Zarbock: Van Nostrand Reinhold Co., New York, 1969.

MACRAME, The Art of Creative Knotting — Virginia I. Harvey: Van Nostrand Reinhold, New York, 1967.

DESIGN ON FABRICS — Meda Parker Johnston and Glen Kaufman: Van Nostrand Reinhold, New York, 1967.

INTRODUCING BATIK — Evelyn Samuel: Watson-Guptill Publications, Cincinnati, 1969.

THE ART OF WEAVING — Else Regensteiner: Van Nostrand Reinhold, New York, 1970.

INTRODUCING DYEING AND PRINTING — Beryl Ash and Anthony Dyson: Watson-Guptill Publications, Cincinnati, 1969.

INTRODUCING ENAMELING — Valery Conway: Watson-Guptill Publications, Cincinnati, 1969.

THE ART OF ENAMELING — Margarete Seeler: Van Nostrand Reinhold, New York, 1969.

ENAMELING, PRINCIPLES AND PRACTICE — Kenneth Bates: World Publishing Co., New York, 1951.

THE TECHNIQUE OF ENAMELING — Geoffrey Clarke, Francis and Ida Feher: Van Nostrand Reinhold, New York, 1967.

PUPPETS, MARIONETTES, MASKS

PUPPET MAKING THROUGH THE GRADES — Grizella Hopper: Davis Publications, Inc., Worcester, Mass., 1966.

HAND PUPPETS AND STRING PUPPETS — Waldo Lanchester: Charles A. Bennett Co., Peoria, Ill., 1953.

INTRODUCING PUPPETRY — Peter Fraser: Watson-Guptill Publications, Cincinnati, 1968.

CREATING AND PRESENTING HAND PUPPETS — John Bodor: Van Nostrand Reinhold Co., New York, 1967.

PRESENTING MARIONETTES — Susan French: Van Nostrand Reinhold Co., New York, 1964.

PUPPETRY TODAY — Helen Binyon: Watson-Guptill Publications, Inc., New York, 1966.

MASKS AND MASK MAKERS — Kari Hunt and Bernice W. Carlson: Abington Press, Nashville, Tenn., 1961.

MASK MAKING, Creative Methods and Techniques — Matthew Baranski: Davis Publications, Inc., Worcester, Mass., 1966.

ART HISTORY

STORY-LIVES OF MASTER ARTISTS — Anna Curtis Chandler: J. B. Lippincott Co., New York, 1953.

MODERN PAINTING — Burton Wasserman: Davis Publications, Inc., Worcester, Mass., 1970.

LOOKING INTO ART — Frank Seiberling: Henry Holt and Co., Inc., New York, 1959.

ART AND CIVILIZATION — Bernard S. Myers: McGraw-Hill Book Co., New York, 1967.

THE STORY OF ART — Ernest Gombrich: Phaidon Publishing Co., New York, 1954.

ART AS IMAGE AND IDEA — Edmund B. Feldman: Prentice-Hall, Englewood Cliffs, N.J., 1967.

THE STORY OF MODERN ART — Sheldon Cheney: Viking Press, New York, 1951.

AMERICAN NEGRO ART — Cedric Dover: New York Graphic Society, New York, 1960.

THE COLOR SLIDE PROGRAM OF THE WORLD'S ART — McGraw-Hill Book Co., New York.

HOW ARTISTS WORK — Pierre Belves and Francois Mathey: The Lion Press, New York, 1968.

ENJOYING THE WORLD OF ART — Pierre Belves and Francois Mathey, The Lion Press, New York, 1966.

THE ENCYCLOPEDIA OF ART — Eleanor C. Munro: Golden Press, Inc., New York, 1961.

THE ARTIST IN AMERICA, Compiled by The Editors of Art in America: W. W. Norton and Co., Inc., New York, 1967.

THE MANY WAYS OF SEEING — Janet Gaylord Moore: The World Publishing Co., New York, 1967.

EL ENCANTO DE UN PUEBLO (The Magic of a People) — Alexander Girard: Viking Press, New York, 1968.

45 CONTEMPORARY MEXICAN ARTISTS — Virginia Stewart: Stanford University Press, Stanford, California.

TWENTIETH CENTURY ART — Michael Batterberry: McGraw-Hill Book Co., New York.

The following titles are outstanding as motivational materials in relation to masks, totems, relief sculpture, sculpture-in-the-round, ornamentation, ceremonial objects. Each book is exceptionally well illustrated.

THE ART OF AFRICA, Tribal Masks — Erich Herold: Drury House, London, England, 1967.

EGYPTIAN MYTHOLOGY — Veronica Ions: Hamlyn House, Middlesex, England, 1968.

NORTH AMERICAN INDIAN MYTHOLOGY — Cottie Burland: Hamlyn House, Middlesex, England, 1968.

AFRICAN MYTHOLOGY — Geoffrey Parrinder: Hamlyn House, Middlesex, England, 1967.

OCEANIC MYTHOLOGY — Roslyn Poignant: Hamlyn House, Middlesex, England, 1967.

GREEK MYTHOLOGY — John Pinsent: Hamlyn House, Middlesex, England, 1969.

INDIAN MYTHOLOGY — Veronica Ions: Hamlyn House, Middlesex, England, 1967.

MEXICAN AND CENTRAL AMERICAN MYTHOLOGY — Irene Nicholson: Hamlyn House, Middlesex, England, 1967.

ENVIRONMENT

ELEMENTS OF THE ART OF ARCHITECTURE — William Muschenheim: Viking Press, New York, 1964.

DESIGN OF CITIES — Edmund N. Bacon: Viking Press, New York, 1967.

ARCHITECTURE TODAY AND TOMORROW — Cranston Jones: McGraw-Hill Book Co., New York, 1966.

SPACE, TIME AND ARCHITECTURE — Sigfried Giedion: Harvard University Press, Cambridge, Mass., 1956.

FACE OF THE METROPOLIS — Martin Myerson: Random House, New York, 1963.

ARCHITECTURE, City Sense — Theodore Crosby: Van Nostrand Reinhold Co., New York, 1965.

THE DEATH AND LIFE OF GREAT AMERICAN CITIES — Jane Jacobs: Random House, Inc., 1961.

Films

DRAWING
CRAYON, 20 minutes, color, A.C.I.

CRAYON RESIST, 6 minutes, color, Bailey-Film Associates.

INTRODUCTION TO GESTURE DRAWING, 12½ minutes, color, Film Associates of California.

INTRODUCTION TO CONTOUR DRAWING, 12 minutes, color, Film Associates of California.

PAINTING
EXPLORING IN PAINT, 11 minutes, color, Bailey-Film Associates.

FINGER PAINTING, 10 minutes, color, International Film Bureau.

GRAPHICS
HOW TO MAKE A LINOLEUM BLOCK PRINT, 14 minutes, black & white, Bailey-Film Associates.

HOW TO MAKE A SILK SCREEN PRINT, 20 minutes, black & white, Almanac Films.

DESIGN
BEGONE DULL CARE, 8 minutes, color, International Film Bureau. Motivational presentation of colors, forms, figures and lines, interpreting accompanying music.

BLUE AND ORANGE, 15 minutes, color, Contemporary Films. Adventure of two bouncing balls that explore and play like children, expressing curiosity, adventure, joy.

DESIGN, 10 minutes, color, Bailey-Film Associates. Shapes, repeated shapes and distortion in design.

FIDDLE DE DEE, 4 minutes, color, International Film Bureau. Motivational; color combinations.

GUMBASIA, 4 minutes, color, Creative Film Shell Oil Company. Motivational presentation of illusions of mass and space.

DISCOVERING COLOR, 15 minutes, color, Film Associates of California.

DISCOVERING COMPOSITION IN ART, 16 minutes, color, Film Associates of California.

DISCOVERING CREATIVE PATTERN, 17 minutes, color, Film Associates of California.

DISCOVERING DARK AND LIGHT, 18 minutes, color, Film Associates of California.

DISCOVERING HARMONY IN ART, 16 minutes, color, Film Associates of California.

DISCOVERING LINE, 17 minutes, color, Film Associates of California.

DISCOVERING TEXTURE, 20 minutes, color, Film Associates of California.

LINE, 10 minutes, color, Portafilms.

PRINT WITH A BRAYER, 8 minutes, color, Bailey-Film Associates.

PRINTS, 15 minutes, color, A.C.I.

SPACE, 10 minutes, color, Bailey-Film Associates.

PAPIER—MÂCHÉ, 15 minutes, color, A.C.I. Papier-Mâché shows the potential of the medium, and gives children the confidence to explore it.

POSTERS, 15 minutes, color, A.C.I. Demonstrates a number of techniques for poster-making including cut paper, collage, tempera paint, crayon resist and silkscreen.

PRINTS, 15 minutes, color, A.C.I. Presents a number of print-making processes that may be carried out with the use of simple, readily available materials.

PUPPETS, 15 minutes, color, A.C.I. Presents a number of puppet-making techniques varying in their levels of difficulty.

SILKSCREEN, 15 minutes, color, A.C.I. (Demonstrates the use of various materials for making stencils including paper, crayon, found objects, and silkscreen film).

THE ALPHABET IN ART, 13 minutes, color, Bailey-Film Associates. Variety of tools and materials that can be used in lettering.

INTRODUCTION TO SCULPTURE METHODS, 18½ minutes, color, Bailey-Film Associates. Sculpture created by three general methods: carving, modeling, and assembling.

EXPLORING RELIEF PRINTMAKING, 12 minutes, color, Film Associates of California. (Four main types of relief prints are explained and shown.)

MASKS, 12 minutes, color, Film Associates of California. The world's greatest collection of masks, both primitive and modern, is presented.

THE PURPLE TURTLE, 15 minutes, color, A.C.I. Captures the excitement that art offers young children.

SCULPTURE

HOW TO MAKE PAPIER-MÂCHÉ ANIMALS, 20 minutes, color, Bailey-Film Associates.

PAPER IN THE ROUND, 10 minutes, color, McGraw Hill.

PAPER SCULPTURE, 6 minutes, color, International Film Bureau.

THREE-DIMENSIONAL DESIGN

ART FROM SCRAP, 5 minutes, color, International Film Bureau.

WOOD CONSTRUCTION FOR BEGINNERS, 14 minutes, black & white, Tabletoppers.

CRAFTS

CERAMIC ART: THE COIL METHOD, 21 minutes, color, McGraw Hill.

THE CHILD AS A POTTER, 17 minutes, color, Classroom Film Dist.

LINES IN RELIEF, WOODCUT & BLOCK PRINTING, 12 minutes, color, Encyclopaedia Britannica Films.

LOOM WEAVING, 10 minutes, color, International Film Bureau.

SURFACE DECORATION, 9 minutes, black & white, Tabletopper.

CLAY, 15 minutes, color, A.C.I. Introduces the natural plastic material as an art medium of great versatility and almost limitless potential.

STITCHERY, 15 minutes, color, A.C.I. Encompasses the techniques of embroidery, needlepoint and appliqué.

ART APPRECIATION

EXPRESSIONISM, 6 minutes, color, Bailey-Film Associates.

THE MAGIC MIRROR, 28 minutes, color, Association Films. Great art masterpieces showing how the artist interprets the world around him.

MEANING IN MODERN PAINTING, PART I, 23 minutes, color, Encyclopaedia Britannica.

MEANING IN MODERN PAINTING, PART II, 17 minutes, color, Encyclopaedia Britannica.

TREASURES OF TIME: PAINTING, 20 minutes, color, International Film Bureau.

TREASURES OF TIME: SCULPTURE, 20 minutes, color, International Film Bureau.

TWENTIETH CENTURY ART, 20 minutes, color, Alemann Films.

FROM THE CIRCUS TO THE MOON, 15 minutes, color, Contemporary Films.

ART IN OUR WORLD, 11 minutes, color, Bailey-Film Associates.

DISCOVERING HARMONY IN ART, 16 minutes, color, Film Associates of California.

MICHELANGELO, 30 minutes, color, Encyclopaedia Britannica Films.

Loops

HESTER AND ASSOCIATES, Dallas, Texas. Single-concept films related to awareness, design, art processes, painting.

Prints

SHOREWOOD ART PROGRAMS FOR EDUCATION, New York. Comprehensive collection of the world's greatest masterpieces coordinated with text material.

Periodicals

SCHOOL ARTS, Davis Publications, Inc., Worcester, Massachusetts.
CREATIVE CRAFTS, Oxford Press, Los Angeles, California.
DESIGN, Design Publishing Co., Columbus, Ohio.

Acknowledgements

The authors wish to express their sincere thanks to the following:

Rosemary Beymer, Director, Department of Art Education, Kansas City Public Schools, Missouri; R. A. Yoder, Art Director, Waynesboro Public Schools, Virginia; Sarita R. Rainey, Supervisor of Art, Montclair Public Schools, New Jersey; Leven C. Leatherbury, Specialist in Art Education, San Diego City Schools, California; Marie Larkin, Supervisor of Art, St. Louis Public Schools, Missouri; Ruth M. Ebken, Associate Director of Instruction, Art, Pittsburgh Public Schools, Pennsylvania; E. Frances Crimm, Art Supervisor, Greensboro Public Schools, North Carolina; Richard Sperisen, Arts Consultant and Director of School Design, San Mateo City School District, California; Theodore P. Foote, Assistant Superintendent-Instruction, Allegany County, Maryland; Vincent J. Popolizio, Chief, Bureau of Art Education, State Education Department, Albany, New York; Peter Smith, art teacher, Hoosick Falls Central School, New York; Rosaline Herstein, Supervisor, Creative Arts, Department of Mental Health, Boston, Massachusetts; John Conner Hill, art teacher, Rough Rock Demonstration School, Chinle, Arizona; Dorothy Murdock, art teacher, Middletown Township Schools, Belford, New Jersey; David Robbins, Director, Project Create, Hartford, Connecticut; John C. Nerreau, Director of Art, Bridgeport, Connecticut; Mabel A. Thompson, Jackson School, Birmingham, Alabama; Doris Standerfer, Professor of Art and Education, San Jose College, California; Phyllis Nelson, W. T. Clarke High School, Westbury, New York; Edith Moore, Principal, Pat Neff Elementary School, Houston, Texas; Ted Couch, Art Consultant, Fort Worth Public Schools, Texas; Janetta Smith, Elementary Art Supervisor, Spring Branch School District, Houston, Texas; Marjorie Gudgen, Director of Art Education, Amarillo, Texas; Margaret Ivy, Art Supervisor, North East School District, San Antonio, Texas; Velma Jo Whitfield, Art Supervisor, San Angelo Public Schools, Texas; Sally Mogford, first grade teacher, Midland Public Schools, Texas; Mary Chatham, Principal, and Ramona Nance, kindergarten teacher, Herod Elementary School, Houston, Texas. The following from the Houston Independent School District, Texas: Mary P. Temple, Director of Art; Frances Homeyer, Art Consultant; Richard Bruns, Director of Program Development; Bernice Marshall, Art Consultant; Alice Webb, Art Consultant; Virginia Rayburn, second grade teacher; Early Adams, Arts and Crafts teacher; Maurine Pagan, kindergarten teacher; Janis Giles, fifth grade teacher; Pat Robertson, fourth grade teacher; Virginia Collins, elementary music teacher; Delois Garland, first grade teacher; Betty Ramazetti, Art Consultant.

And to the supervisory staff of the Baltimore City Public Schools, Maryland: Richard L. Micherdzinski, Director of Art; Helga Hermann, Supervisor of Art, Elementary Schools; Elizabeth K. Walton, Art Specialist, Elementary Schools; Arthur Pierce, Art Specialist, Elementary Schools; Helen Speck, Art Specialist, Elementary Schools.

And: Mrs. Frederick Buxton, Curator of Exhibitions, Museum of Fine Arts, Houston, Texas; Mrs. Braxton Thompson, Docent Coordinator, Museum of Fine Arts, Houston, Texas; Sebastian Adler, Director, Contemporary Arts Museum, Houston, Texas; Arthur E. Smith, photographer, Houston, Texas; Janet Fox, Art Education, University of Houston, Texas; Beth Mathis, Art Education, Houston Baptist College, Texas.

Please remember that this is a library book,
and that it belongs only temporarily to each
person who uses it. Be considerate. Do
not write in this, or any, library book.